At the EDGE of the PRECIPICE

At the EDGE
of the PRECIPICE

HENRY CLAY *and the* COMPROMISE
That SAVED *the* UNION

ROBERT V. REMINI

BASIC
BOOKS
A Member of the Perseus Books Group
New York

Books published by Basic Books are available at special discounts for
bulk purchases in the United States by corporations, institutions, and
other organizations. For more information, please contact the Special
Markets Department at the Perseus Books Group, 2300 Chestnut
Street, Suite 200, Philadelphia, PA 19103, or call (800) 810-4145,
ext. 5000, or e-mail special.markets@perseusbooks.com.
Editorial Production by the Book Factory.

The image of Henry Clay on page ix appears with permission from the
United States Senate Commission on Art.

Library of Congress Cataloging-in-Publication Data

Remini, Robert Vincent, 1921-
    At the edge of the precipice : Henry Clay and the compromise that
saved the Union / Robert V. Remini.—1st ed.
        p. cm.
    Includes bibliographical references and index.
    ISBN 978-0-465-01288-6 (alk. paper)
    1. Clay, Henry, 1777-1852. 2. Compromise of 1850. 3. United
States—Politics and government—1815-1861. 4. United States—Politics
and government—Philosophy. 5. Slavery—United States—History—
19th century. I. Title.
    E423.R46 2010
    973.5—dc22

                                    2010001309

10 9 8 7 6 5 4 3 2 1

For Ruth

CONTENTS

*Henry Clay speaking in the
Old Senate Chamber.*

This 7 by 11 foot, one-hundred-pound portrait of Henry Clay speaking in the Old Senate Chamber, and surrounded left to right by several of his friends and colleagues—William H. Seward, R. M. T. Hunter, Robert Letcher, General Winfield Scott, George Robertson, Daniel Webster, Joseph Rogers Underwood, Sam Houston, John Crittenden, Lewis Cass, Thomas Hart Benton, and Stephen A. Douglas—was painted by Phineas Staunton in 1867 for a competition sponsored by the state of Kentucky to memorialize the Great Compromiser. The painting eventually wound up in the Le Roy Historical Society in upstate New York and lay, virtually unknown, for fifty years in a storage room. Amy Elizabeth Burton, an art historian in the Curator's Office of the U.S. Senate, discovered the painting and arranged for its removal to the Senate. The painting was torn and covered with dirt and grime; it took seventeen months for the painting and its frame to be restored. It now hangs on a wall in a staircase leading to the Senate chamber in the U.S. Capitol. It is an excellent likeness of Clay, which very few people have seen, and shows him pointing to a document bearing the date 1851.

PREFACE

In 1850, a decade prior to the election of Abraham Lincoln, the secession of southern states, and the firing on Fort Sumter in April 1861, the Union of American states came close to being irreparably smashed. Had that happened, it is arguable that two or more independent nations would have been formed, thus permanently dissolving what was once the United States of America. And had war resulted between the free states of the North and the slaves states of the South in 1850, rather than a decade later, it seems likely that the more militant South would have defeated the much weaker North and made good its separation from the Union. Once the great men of the antebellum era passed away—men such as Andrew Jackson, Henry Clay, Daniel Webster, and John C. Calhoun—the nation lacked individuals in positions of power who were passionately devoted to the Union, men possessing genuine leadership ability who could find solutions to the crises that arose repeatedly over the issue of slavery and thereby threatened the liberty of all. Throughout the decade of the 1850s, the best the nation could offer to stand at the head of government were such figures as Millard Fillmore, Franklin Pierce, and James Buchanan, not one of whom could have provided the statesmanship by which the Union could be kept intact.

Fortunately, in 1850, the crisis was averted. It was averted because there were a number of men in Congress who were willing to compromise—and not simply on one issue, like slavery, but on many related issues that divided North and South, such as congressional control of the territories, the admission of California, the New Mexico boundary, and the Texas debt.

In this book I seek to explain the extent of the crisis, its long history, why it was so catastrophic, its importance for the nation, and its results. I also seek to show the importance of compromise in resolving problems of great magnitude in the history of the country. It has proven time and time again that little of lasting importance can be accomplished without a willingness on the part of all involved to seek to accommodate one another's needs and demands. This point is especially important today when the nation faces myriad problems, both foreign and domestic, that defy easy solution, and that will, in all likelihood, require both major political parties to agree to compromise their differences. With severe economic problems that threaten to pitch the nation into a deep recession; with other domestic issues, such as health care, energy, immigration, and social concerns such as abortion and gay marriage; with wars in the Middle East that verge on escalation throughout the region; and with terrorism rampant around the globe, compromise on the part of this nation's political leaders, and the leaders of other countries, becomes all the more necessary.

The Compromise of 1850 is a prime example of how close this nation came to a catastrophic smash-up, and the way the power brokers of that period avoided that disaster—just in time. The Compromise gave the North ten years to build its industrial strength and enable it to overpower the South when war finally broke out. It also gave the North ten years to find a leader who could save the Union. His name: Abraham Lincoln.

1

COMPROMISE IN THE
NATION'S EARLY HISTORY

The Founders of this nation—men of the Enlightenment—
understood the importance of compromise in achieving
important goals. Because they put together a bundle of compromises that resolved their many problems, they succeeded in
writing the Constitution of the United States, which created a
republic that has survived for more than two hundred years.
Their compromises produced a Union of thirteen separate, sovereign, independent states. They compromised on the structure
of the legislature and the extent of its duties; on the method by
which members of Congress would be elected; and on the powers delegated to each branch of government. They compromised over the demands of large and small states, and they
compromised on the existence of slavery and the role it would
play in the distribution of representatives in the lower house of

AT THE EDGE OF THE PRECIPICE

Congress. Indeed, the Constitution is one long collection of compromises.

When the Founders finished their work and submitted it to the people of the several states for their ratification, they hoped that their own and succeeding generations would also understand the value and importance of compromise and how essential it was in resolving conflict and ensuring peace. And yet, just thirty years later, the Union almost came apart.

———

The origins of the crisis of 1850 lay in decisions made nearly half a century earlier. To start, President Thomas Jefferson in 1803 purchased the Louisiana Territory from France—an immense area that doubled the size of the country—that triggered a titanic battle in Congress in 1819 when Missouri, carved from this territory, applied for admission into the Union as a slave state. Missouri was the first territory to be located completely west of the Mississippi River. Unfortunately, if granted, this request for admission would upset the balance between the number of free and slave states in the Union, tilting the number in favor of the slave states. Northerners reacted angrily. To rectify this problem, Representative James Tallmadge Jr. of New York proposed amending the enabling act that would admit Missouri as a state so that, in time, Missouri would become a free state. His amendment prohibited the further introduction of slaves into the territory and would free those slave children born in Missouri upon reaching the age of twenty-five.

Southerners exploded with indignation. This obvious ploy on the part of northerners to restrict the expansion of slavery was not only dastardly, they cried, but a violation of the Constitution. Northerners were not content with the Northwest Ordinance of 1787 forbidding slavery north of the Ohio River, southerners ranted. Now they argued for the right of Congress to legislate on slavery in the territories and the right to abolish slavery for the entire territory of the Louisiana Purchase. On the floor of Congress, Representative Thomas W. Cobb of Georgia shook his fist at Tallmadge. "If you persist," he screamed, "the Union will be dissolved. You have kindled a fire which all the waters of the ocean cannot put out, which seas of blood can only extinguish."

"Let it come," shouted Tallmadge in response.[1]

The Speaker of the House, Henry Clay of Kentucky, condemned the Tallmadge amendment. A slave owner himself, he nevertheless regarded slavery as an evil that betrayed American values of liberty and free government. He had worked diligently, but without success, to convince Kentuckians to change their state constitution and provide for gradual emancipation. He was a leader of the American Colonization Society, which sought to win freedom for slaves and then colonize them in Africa.[2] Chosen president of the society in 1836, he remained in that office until the end of his life. And yet, despite his views about slavery, Clay opposed the Tallmadge amendment because he believed that it violated the Constitution, which protected the property of all citizens. The amendment would deprive Missourians of their slave property and therefore contradicted the fundamental law of the country.

Clay's role in finding a solution to the Missouri crisis demonstrates how well he understood the importance and the meaning of compromise. As he said many times, compromise involves victory for both sides of a dispute. There can be no losers—or winners. Each side must feel that it has gained something that is essential to its interest as a result of the compromise. To achieve that goal, each side must surrender something important to the opposing side. Both can then claim victory.

Presiding over the House of Representatives during this crisis, Clay behaved not as a director of legislative traffic, as previous Speakers had done, but as the controlling hand in managing the business of the House. He was a man of commanding grace, which compensated for the fact that he was a singularly unattractive looking man. He had a high forehead, a protruding nose, small blue eyes, and a wide mouth that looked like a long slash across his face. But when he spoke he could be electrifying. His enthusiasm and total involvement in what he was saying and his frequent majestic flights of oratory mesmerized his audience. At times his entire six-foot frame seemed to move in concert with the words he spoke.

Although only forty-two years old at the time of the Missouri crisis, Clay was already an experienced politician. Born in Virginia on April 12, 1777, Clay studied law with George Wythe, the most learned jurist in Virginia; was admitted to the bar on November 6, 1797; moved to Kentucky, where his intelligence and abilities were quickly recognized; and won election to the state legislature. In 1806, although still under the constitutionally mandated age of thirty, he was elected to the U.S. Senate to finish out the term of a senator who had resigned. In 1810, he was again sent to Washington to replace a senator who resigned. Clay served in that position until 1811.

But in August 1810, Clay was elected to the U.S. House of Representatives, and because his many talents were already known in Washington, he was chosen Speaker on the first ballot, an extraordinary feat. And it was in that office that he attempted to put together a compromise that would end the Missouri controversy.

The debate over the Tallmadge amendment became quite heated. The question of slavery, and particularly the presumption by northerners that Congress could legislate on the issue and restrict its growth, set off a brouhaha on the floor of the House that agitated everyone. "The words, civil war, and disunion," Clay informed Adam Beatty, a close friend, "are uttered almost without emotion," and one senator declared he would prefer civil war and disunion if the amendment failed.[3]

A possible solution—although a partial one—arose during the following congressional session, when Maine, the northern district of Massachusetts, applied in 1820 to become a separate and free state of the Union. Maine's admission into the Union would resolve the problem of keeping a balance of free states and slave states. Clay realized this at once and publicly declared that unless Missouri was admitted unconditionally, there was no possibility of Maine winning statehood.

In the Senate, which was having its own verbal contest over the crisis, the two separate admission bills or enabling acts (Missouri's and Maine's) were united into a single bill, and a further amendment was put forward by Senator Jesse B. Thomas of Illinois to prohibit the further extension of slavery into the territory of the Louisiana Purchase north of 36°30'—with the exception of Missouri, since most of that area was situated north of the line.

This Thomas amendment provided the happy result of satisfying both northerners and southerners while at the same time forcing each to make a concession. It validated the claim by northerners that Congress had the right and authority to restrict the spread of slavery in the territories while granting southerners access to an area of the Louisiana Purchase below 36°30'. Southerners knew that climate conditions were such that slavery would never survive in the frigid north so there was no problem in allowing this restriction. But the compromise did permit the expansion of slavery below the line. Thus, North and South each achieved what it wanted and did so by granting concessions to the other side.

When this Senate bill came to the House, Speaker Clay, who supported the Thomas amendment, descended from his chair on the dais and spoke from the well of the House. And he spoke for four hours, arguing eloquently that the future of the Union was at stake and the members of the House were honor-bound to do all in their power to preserve it. Besides demonstrating his skill at oratory, he wheedled, cajoled, and even threatened his colleagues in the attempt to win passage of the bill in the lower chamber.[4] He also "wielded the powers of pathos in a manner so sublime and touching, that . . . half the House were in tears," reported one newspaper.[5]

With such verbal power behind it, the compromise passed, providing in three separate bills a free Maine, a slave Missouri, and no slavery north of 36°30', except for Missouri. President

Monroe, who had worked behind the scenes to win passage of the compromise, signed the measure on March 6, 1820, and secession was prevented.[6]

But trouble erupted once again. Missouri, as directed by the compromise settlement, forged ahead and wrote a constitution. The settlement further stated that the state government to be created must be "republican" and must not be in conflict with the U.S. Constitution. It was assumed that slavery would be permitted and that the Congress would automatically approve it. But Missouri, outraged over congressional dictation, went further and wrote a constitution requiring its legislature to enact laws that would forbid "free negroes and mulattoes" from entering the state. Since free blacks were citizens in a few states, the Missouri constitution was a clear violation of the U.S. Constitution. The second section of Article IV of the U.S. Constitution states that citizens of any state must be entitled to all privileges and immunities of citizens in the several states.

Naturally, northern congressmen took violent exception to this action and swore to refuse recognition of Missouri as a state when its representatives appeared in Washington. Missouri had failed to perform its part as dictated by the enabling act, they contended, and therefore it was still a territory. But Clay, once again, stepped in and calmed the agitated Congress. He prepared a report calling for the admission of Missouri "upon the fundamental condition" that its legislature would never pass a law preventing "any description of persons" from settling in the state who was or might become a citizen of any state in the Union. The report argued that the rights of free blacks had to be protected. By a vote of 87 to 81, this Second Missouri Compromise, as it was called, passed the House, followed two days later by the Senate.[7]

For his efforts Henry Clay was dubbed "the Great Compromiser" and "the Great Pacificator." The "Constitution of the Union was in danger," said Representative Langdon Cheves of South Carolina, "& has been Saved."[8]

———

Although the Missouri Compromise did prevent secession and civil war in the 1820s, it did not solve the problem of slavery. The fact that the nation had come so close to secession frightened Thomas Jefferson, by then living in retirement. He warned that the incident could very well "burst on us as a tornado." It was, he said, like hearing "a firebell in the night."[9]

That firebell rang louder a year later when Denmark Vesey, a free mulatto, led an army of slaves in Charleston, South Carolina, in a revolt to gain their freedom. They were savagely assaulted by five companies of militia, who put down the rebellion. Ten years later, on August 22, 1831, an even worse uprising occurred at Jerusalem in southeastern Virginia. Nat Turner led a hundred fellow slaves in a bid for freedom and murdered sixty whites, virtually wiping out the entire white community. The local constabulary responded and in a mad act of revenge slaughtered every Negro they encountered, guilty or not. Several hundred blacks died in the bloodbath.

These rebellions were not the only ones. In the 1820s and 1830s there were any number of race riots in America, including several in the nation's capital. Although there had been abolitionists back in the colonial era, especially among Quakers, a movement to win the freedom of slaves was now energized by the zeal for reform that emerged during the years when Andrew Jackson was president (1829–1837). A Second Great Awakening occurred following the War of 1812, galvanizing thousands of Americans who sought to revolutionize living and working conditions throughout the country. These zealots found evil in society and set about the task of rooting it out wherever it existed. One of the worst institutions in the United States, they declared, was slavery, the so-called "peculiar institution," a euphemism that many southerners preferred to use when discussing the issue.

To address this abomination, abolitionists organized themselves. They founded the American Antislavery Society in 1833, which involved the scheduling of antislavery meetings, the creation of an underground railroad to assist runaway slaves to escape to freedom, and a push for the passage of "personal liberty laws" forbidding state officials from assisting in the capture and return of runaway slaves. Several newspapers were established to advance the cause, such as the *Genius of Universal Emancipation*, a Baltimore journal edited by Benjamin Lundy. A more influential and fiery newspaper was *The Liberator*, edited by William Lloyd Garrison, who claimed that because the Constitution recognized slavery in the United States, it was nothing more than "an agreement with hell and a covenant with death." Worse, he labeled George Washington a thief and kidnapper who was "now in hell."[10]

The power of slavery to provoke sectional hostility was such that President Jackson feared it could threaten the Union and jeopardize democracy. "Look, I pray you," he said to one concerned group in 1835, "at the efforts which are making to array one section of the Union against the other. It is in this aspect that the movements of the abolitionists become fearful and portentous." They claimed to be motivated by "religion," he declared, "the cause of humanity and . . . the right of the human race," but everyone, "upon sober reflection, will see that nothing but mischief can come from these improper assaults upon the feelings and rights of others."[11]

The Missouri controversy had already demonstrated the existence of sectional discord. To many Americans, it seemed more than likely that some simple resolution or issue could arise in Congress that could produce another crisis that would touch off a floor fight and imperil the Union. Whatever the issue, most everyone believed that slavery would be found lurking behind it. And sure enough, it came with a quarrel over the tariff, which quickly broadened into a question of whether a state could nullify a federal law, and even secede from the Union, if its grievances were rejected, leaving the state, said some southerners, with no recourse but to secede from the Union or fight if necessary to defend its rights.

This second explosion in Congress occurred in the late 1820s and had its roots in laws passed fifteen years earlier. With the close of the War of 1812, the industrialization of the North brought demands for a protective tariff to safeguard American products from foreign competition. Earlier, tariffs had been enacted solely to raise revenue, but in 1816 Congress passed the first protective tariff. Henry Clay became a leading advocate of what he labeled "the American System," which called for protective tariffs, a sound credit and currency system directed by a central bank, and the enactment of internal improvements such as the building of roads, canals, bridges, and railroads.

Southerners took exception to the tariff law, claiming it favored northern industry at the expense of southern interests and was therefore discriminatory. They protested that they sold their cotton worldwide on an open market but had to buy manufactured products, such as clothes, on a closed market in the North protected by tariff legislation. To their minds, the federal government was assisting one section of the country while penalizing another—and that was unfair and unconstitutional.

Matters came to a head during the presidential election campaign of 1828. Andrew Jackson's friends and supporters in Congress decided to enact a new tariff specifically intended to benefit those states that Old Hickory needed to win. The tariff bill they proposed would punish states like those of New England that supported the opposition candidate, John Quincy Adams. It levied a duty of 10 cents per gallon on imported molasses and distilled spirits. Then the duty on hemp and flax was fixed at $45 per ton, to be increased annually until it reached $60 as a maximum. The duty on sail duck, a type of canvas, was established at 9 cents per square yard. On raw wool they proposed a duty of 7 cents per pound, plus a 40 percent ad valorem rate, which would be increased each year until it amounted to 50 percent. But on manufactured wool, a most important industry in New England, the rates were disproportionately low and involved a complicated schedule that did not begin to meet the needs of the manufacturers.

Representative Silas Wright Jr. of New York, a henchman of Senator Martin Van Buren, one of Jackson's most ardent champions, explained the logic of the proposal. "Why did we frame the bill as we did?" he wrote to his colleagues in New York. "Because we had put the duties upon all kinds of woolen cloths as high *as our own friends* in Pennsylvania, Kentucky & Ohio would vote them. Why did we put the duties on Molasses so high? Because Pennsylvania and our friends west of that state required it to induce them to go for the woolens. The Hemp and flax duty was also inserted for the same reasons, and the duty on Irons are the Sine qua non with Pennsylvania."[12]

Northern members of the House, particularly those from New England, took one look at this lopsided monstrosity and bellowed their opposition. Henry Clay guessed that the authors did not "really desire the passage of their own measure."[13] They wrote it to force the New England representatives into voting against it. Southerners, who disliked all tariffs, would join them to kill the bill. That was the belief of many congressmen.

But Clay was wrong—in fact, the Jacksonians did intend to enact the measure. They expected southern opposition but knew that they need not worry about losing the South in the election. Southern states would never vote for Adams and against Jackson. What the authors of the bill had done was solicit votes from the middle and western states that Old Hickory needed to win the presidency.

The northern opposition wondered what course of action to take. Should they go for the bill or not? Senator Daniel Webster of Massachusetts, an ardent protectionist, asked the same question. "Can we *go* the *hemp*, iron, spirits and molasses for the sake of any woolens bill?"[14] After careful thought they decided that they could and would go for it. Thus the Tariff of 1828 passed and President John Quincy Adams signed it.

Southerners, who wrongly believed that the tariff was responsible for cotton's recent price decline, dubbed this outrage the "Tariff of Abominations" and swore they would take action against it. Vice President John C. Calhoun of South Carolina returned home when Congress adjourned and set about writing an "Exposition and Protest," in which he not only condemned the tariff but advanced the theory that a state could nullify federal law if the law violated the rights of the state. The Tariff of 1828 was just such a law, and unless it was repealed, South Carolina could nullify its execution within its borders. Such "interposition," argued Calhoun, would protect minority rights and prevent the tyranny of the majority. Nullification, he went on, was intended to prevent secession, but if the federal government attempted to coerce a state into complying with the offending law, then the state had the right to withdraw from the Union.

Calhoun's views about states' rights and nullification received a thorough airing in January 30, 1830, when Daniel Webster and Robert Y. Hayne of South Carolina hotly debated them in the Senate. The debate resulted from a seemingly innocuous resolution restricting the future sale of public lands until those already on the market had been sold. The debate between the two men gradually shifted to the rivalry between the North and South and then to the question of slavery. Hayne protested that until the rights of the South were respected and

13

protected, liberty would be jeopardized and there would be constant turmoil in the country. He defended not only slavery and states' rights but also the doctrine of nullification. Only the states were sovereign, he said, and the Union was nothing more than a compact of states.

Webster rose in the chamber and refuted Hayne's impressive speech, insisting that the United States was a Union of people. "I go for the Constitution as it is, and for the Union as it is," he declared. "It is, Sir, the people's Constitution, the people's government, made for the people, made by the people, and answerable to the people." He closed his second reply to Hayne with the ringing words, "Liberty *and* Union, now and forever, one and inseparable."[15]

This debate highlighted the growing antagonism between North and South over slavery and the tariff and their differences over whether the Union consisted principally of states or people.

In an attempt to resolve one of the problems triggering this dispute, Congress passed the Tariff of 1832, which removed some of the abominations of the 1828 law but did not lower rates a significant level. The bill thus remained unacceptable by southern fire-eaters, who demanded total submission to their arguments and demands.

Matters came to a head when the governor of South Carolina, James Hamilton Jr., called a special session of the legislature, which in turn ordered the election of a convention to meet and take appropriate action. The convention assembled on November 19, 1832, and five days later passed an Ordinance of Nullification by a vote of 136 to 20, declaring the tariffs of 1828 and 1832 "null, void, and no law, nor binding on South Carolina." It forbade the collection of duties after February 1, 1833, and warned that if the federal government attempted to coerce the state into compliance, South Carolina would secede and "forthwith proceed to organize a separate Government."[16]

At this point President Jackson stepped in and issued a sharp warning to the nullifiers in his native state. His Proclamation of December 10 spoke directly to the people of South Carolina and assured them that he would not tolerate defiance of federal law. He had taken an oath to enforce the laws of the land, and "by the eternal," he would do it, even if it meant resorting to violence. "Those who told you that you might peacefully prevent their execution deceived you," he wrote. "Their object is disunion. But be not deceived by names. Disunion by armed force is *treason*. Are you really ready to incur its guilt. . . . On your unhappy State will inevitably fall all the evils of the conflict you force upon the Government of your country."[17]

Quite naturally, the Proclamation was greeted by nullifiers in South Carolina with "scorn & contempt as the mad ravings of a drivelling dotard." But in the North it elicited widespread praise. "The President's proclamation," wrote Richard Rush, "gives great satisfaction to the liberal and patriotic of all parties, hereabouts. . . . May it accomplish its good ends."[18]

Not relying exclusively on the verbal power of his Proclamation, Jackson prepared to use military force if his warning went unheeded. He notified the naval base at Norfolk to prepare a squadron of warships to proceed to Charleston for the possibility of preventing civil strife, and he alerted fort commanders in South Carolina to be on the lookout for a ground attack. Furthermore, he rushed five hundred stand of muskets along with "corresponding equipment" to Fort Pinckney, which he thought might be the first installation to be assaulted. And he directed several thousand troops under the command of General Winfield Scott to be stationed along the Carolina border. Jackson also summoned the aid of Unionists in South Carolina, particularly Joel Poinsett, former minister to Mexico, to assist in putting down rebellion. Poinsett kept Jackson regularly informed about what was happening in his state. "We had rather die," he wrote, "than submit to the tyranny [of the nullifiers]." Jackson immediately responded, "I fully concur with you in your views of Nullification. It leads directly to civil war and bloodshed and deserves the execration of every friend of the country." The government, he said, was behind Poinsett and his fellow Unionists. "I repeat to the union men again, fear not, the union will be preserved and treason and rebellion put down, when and where it may shew its monster head."[19]

Jackson girded for war. When a state attempts to nullify constitutional law and thereby destroy the Union, he said, the "balance of the people composing the union have a perfect right to coerce them to obedience." He signaled an alert to the secretary of war, Lewis Cass. "We must be prepared for the crisis." The moment they heard that the South Carolina legislature had carried its "rebellious ordinance into effect," they "must be prepared to act." And to Martin Van Buren, his vice president–elect, he added, "If South Carolina raises an army of twelve thousand men, I will order thirty thousand to execute the law." This was not the time "to temporize or falter."[20]

As Jackson prepared for war, the nullifiers prepared to resist. The South Carolina legislature asked Hayne to write a resolution to the people of the state warning them that their liberty was in jeopardy and asking them to be ready to fight for their freedom and their property. At the same time, the Unionists in the state armed themselves. They even sought to raise and equip a voluntary force, which Jackson supported. They held a secret meeting to make the necessary arrangements, and when told that Jackson was not afraid to denounce nullification as "treason and rebellion," some of them shouted, "*Enough. What have we to fear, we are right, and God and Old Hickory are with us.*"

It certainly seemed that civil war could not be avoided. In January 1833, General Winfield Scott reportedly wrote to the secretary of war "saying that blood would be shed and that he did not believe any thing could prevent it."[21]

In order to protect the military in the coming conflict with constitutional legality, Jackson decided to go to Congress and ask that it "cloathe our officers and marshall" with necessary authority to engage in acts of war in executing the laws and apprehending those guilty of treason. And he said he needed this authority before February 1, which was the date the Nullification Ordinance set for prohibiting the collection of the tariff duties. Of course, he could act on his own authority, he added, but then he would be branded a "tyrant." On January 16, 1833, he sent Congress his Force Bill message, formally requesting authority to deploy the military to put down armed rebellion. Friends of the administration called the Force Bill a "collection bill," but the nullifiers labeled it a "bloody bill" and a "war bill."[22]

Although Jackson feverishly worked to ready the nation for war, he understood that his first responsibility was to avoid bloodshed if at all possible. To that end he sought to build a moral force around the country to support his position by repeatedly reminding the nation that laws must be obeyed by all citizens, and that no one had the right to pick and choose which laws to obey and which to disobey or disregard. He also encouraged the creation of a volunteer force in South Carolina as a counterweight to the nullifiers.

Most important of all, Jackson planned to do something about lowering the tariff, the single piece of legislation that had triggered the conflict. In his fourth State of the Union address to Congress, on December 4, 1832, the president emphasized the importance of reducing tariff rates. But knowing how long it would take for any bill to work itself through two houses, especially since any proposal had to be written and then approved by slow-moving committees, he directed his secretary of the treasury, Louis McLane, to save time and effort by preparing a bill that could be quickly shepherded through Congress.

McLane immediately set to work, and by mid-December 1832, just as the confrontation with South Carolina was reaching a point of near-collision, a new tariff bill was ready for consideration by Congress. It was delivered to the chairman of the House Ways and Means Committee, Gulian C. Verplanck of New York, with a request that he move it through his committee and onto the floor of the House as quickly as possible. Jackson later referred to it as a tariff bill prepared by McLane under the President's careful supervision. Known as the Verplanck bill, it was introduced in the House on January 8, 1833, the eighteenth anniversary of the Battle of New Orleans, a date at that time virtually equivalent with the Fourth of July.[23]

Jackson expected passage of both the Force Bill and this new tariff at the same time. It was a carrot-and-stick approach, and although the stick was plainly revealed, it was done without threats or any promise of violence. If conflict were to develop, said Jackson, the South Carolinians would have to initiate it. "I have determined," he told the Congress, "to spare no effort to discharge the duty which in this conjuncture is devolved upon me," namely, to enforce the laws of the country. "I . . . solemnly proclaim that the Constitution and the laws are supreme and the Union indissoluble."[24]

According to the terms of the Verplanck bill, tariff duties would be cut by 50 percent, back to approximately the rates of the first protective Tariff of 1816 as amended in 1824. However, duties on a few goods were raised, and some goods, such as coffee and tea, were removed from the free list. The reductions would take place during a two-year period, with half going into effect in 1834 and half in 1835.[25] It was not exactly the kind of reform that Jackson had advocated (he wanted to end protectionism altogether), but it at least addressed some of South Carolina's grievances and was intended as a gesture of friendship. But to protectionists it was totally unacceptable and a clear surrender to the nullifiers. They faced financial disaster if the tariff passed, they insisted.

The most prominent protectionist in the country at the time was Henry Clay, and manufacturers turned to him to find a proper solution to the tariff problem, one that would not only safeguard their financial interests but also spare the country from the impending disaster. Clay had been elected to the U.S. Senate and had gone to Philadelphia to visit a relative. While there he met with a number of men, including his longtime friend and adviser Josiah Johnson and a group of industrialists, who pleaded with him to apply his considerable talents to solving the problem. They felt especially concerned about Jackson's intention to end protectionism.

End protectionism! What a ghastly thought. But it might be necessary if the Union was to be saved. So, after meeting with these men, Clay took only a few days to come up with the draft of a substitute compromise tariff. And that plan was new, innovative, and breathtaking in its scope. He acknowledged the strong differences between those who favored and those who opposed protectionism, and he lamented that their disagreements had brought the country to the edge of civil strife. Thus, in order to prevent bloodshed, he proposed that the existing tariff laws remain in effect until March 3, 1840—seven years hence—at which time all the tariff laws would be repealed. Rates would not be raised in the interim, and then duties would be enacted only to provide such revenues as the government required to operate "without regard to the protection or encouragement of any branch of domestic industry whatever."[26]

It was a fantastic proposal. To save the Union, Clay would sacrifice protectionism after a period of time during which manufacturers could take advantage of the present rates, and then be content with whatever schedule was determined to provide the government with the funds needed to operate. In effect, he declared a truce for seven years. Then, in 1840, protectionism would end. It was a compromise in which both sides would win: Both sides could claim victory because they would achieve their immediate goals. The South would have the end of protectionism to look forward to, and the North would have high rates for the next seven years. But both sides would have to make a sacrifice for the sake of preserving the Union. The South had to live with the present high rates for seven years, and the North would have to accept the ultimate end of protectionism down the road.

Some protectionists questioned Clay's commitment to principle. Was he not the author of the American System, which called for protective tariffs, a sound banking system, and internal improvements? But Clay was never rigid in his ideological thinking. He understood that politics is not about ideological purity or moral self-righteousness. It was about governing, and if politicians could not compromise, they would never govern effectively.

Being wise as well as shrewd, Clay had a backup plan, which he also outlined to the industrialists in Philadelphia. According to this plan, the tariff rates would be repealed immediately and replaced by a new tariff in which all duties on unprotected articles would be abolished. Seven years hence, all duties for protection would cease entirely and a general ad valorem tax would begin to be levied on all importations.[27]

After explaining his two plans to the Philadelphia businessmen, Clay asked for their reaction. They assured him of their support, despite what must have been their disappointment in hearing about the seven-year truce. But like many in America they believed that Clay would one day soon occupy the White House, and they figured that once he was in power he would provide the necessary support to help them build this country into a great industrial powerhouse. So they gave him their unqualified approval for the seven-year plan. As for the alternate, they advised him to wait until he had a chance to discuss it with his southern friends after his return to Washington.

On his way back to the capital from Philadelphia, Clay ran into Daniel Webster and seized the opportunity to tell him of his scheme to settle the crisis. After hearing the details, Webster said he would have none of it. The mere mention of ending protectionism after seven years was enough to convince him that he must oppose any effort to enact the plan into law. And he was sure that three-fourths of the tariff interests in the North would feel the same way.

Clay had better luck when he reached Washington and had a chance to converse with several southern congressmen who did not support the nullifiers but who did demand lower rates in any compromise legislation. Clay explained his two plans and said he offered to surrender the principle of protection in return for "*time.*"

"*Time*," responded Senator John Tyler of Virginia, "is of little importance to us." It was the principle of ending protectionism that he said southerners demanded. But he was so taken with Clay's proposals that he was almost ready to say that the battle was "fought and won." "My fears for the Union are rapidly dissipating," he wrote.[28]

Time in exchange for principle. That was the deal, and a number of southern congressmen rather liked the idea. In addition, Clay reminded them, as if they needed reminding, that President Jackson stood ready to provoke havoc and fight a civil war if they pursued their course of nullification. Jackson, he said, had "marked out two victims—South Carolina and the Tariff—and the only question with him is which shall be first immolated."[29] Having just been defeated by Old Hickory in the presidential election of 1832, Clay looked on the president as a real threat to the country—he once called him a "military chieftain" who endangered the nation's freedom—and he felt an urgency about winning the contest over nullification and the tariff. Such a victory would spare the Union from civil war and block the military chieftain from riding roughshod over South Carolina. Even so, by the start of the new year, 1833, it certainly looked as though a violent confrontation between Jackson and South Carolina was inevitable. The state had no intention of backing off, and the Hero of New Orleans would never retreat. It was not in his nature.

To demonstrate its determination to make good on its demands, South Carolina decided to strengthen its position in Washington. An arrangement was worked out in which Senator Robert Y. Hayne would resign his seat in Congress and replace James Hamilton Jr. as governor, while John C. Calhoun would resign the vice presidency (which he otherwise would have held until March 4, 1834) and take Hayne's place in the Senate. In this way a strong voice would be positioned at the center of the political arena in Washington to explain and defend nullification and fight for states' rights.

So Calhoun—instead of presiding over the Senate and remaining mute—now sat on the floor and prepared to denounce "with passion and excitement" Jackson's determination to drench South Carolina in blood. Once sworn in and seated in the Senate, he demanded recognition and then proceeded to decry the military despotism that the president seemed determined to invoke. "Without provocation," Calhoun thundered, "our Union," during a time of peace, "stands on the eve of dissolution or the verge of a civil war." Obviously, he stormed, "the country had now reached a crisis" and its future seemed bleak.[30]

Jackson scoffed. "Mr. Calhoun let off a little of his ire against me today in the Senate," he told Joel Poinsett, "but was so agitated and confused that he made quite a failure."[31]

The Senate waited to see what would happen next. Clay agreed with the president that the laws of the country had to be enforced, but he had no confidence that Jackson would not abuse his authority and damage, if not annihilate, the freedom of the American people. Clay was ambivalent as to how he should proceed. So while he was considering his options, suddenly, to everyone's surprise, who should step forward as the administration's spokesman in the Senate in defending the Force Bill but that renowned protectionist and nationalist Daniel Webster. A Unionist to his fingertips, he abhorred nullification, and in the next several weeks he and Calhoun verbally wrestled over passage of the "Bloody bill," as the South Carolinian called it, declaring it nothing more than an unconstitutional declaration of war against a sovereign state. Webster, of course, charged Calhoun with ignorance about the nature of the Union. It was not a compact, as the nullifiers insisted, he declared, but a perpetual Union of people.[32]

Clay now rose and added his voice to the great debate. He knew that nullification was a dead issue—which indeed it was. As for South Carolina, he said, "I do not want to disgrace her, nor any member of this Union." If there were any in the chamber who wanted civil war, who wanted to see the blood of their countrymen "spilt," he stormed, "I am not one of them. I wish to see war of no kind, but, above all, I do not desire to see civil war."[33]

So, for the next several weeks, the Senate chamber reverberated with the brilliant oratory of Clay, Calhoun, and Webster, "the Great Triumvirate," as they came to be called.

Although Calhoun did everything in his power to delay or defeat the Force Bill, it came to a vote on February 20 and passed the Senate, 32 to 1. During the voting all the nullifiers in the chamber walked out. John Tyler of Virginia cast the one dissenting vote. He, too, abhorred nullification, but he strongly opposed using force against a sovereign state.

Henry Clay did not vote. Since he was closeted with southerners during the debate, attempting to win support for his compromise, he chose not to record his position on the issue. Naturally, one of the southerners whom Clay consulted at length was John C. Calhoun—and he was quite open about it. Indeed, so obvious was his intention that even Jacksonians understood what was going on and commented on it. Prior to the final vote on the Force Bill, Senator Silas Wright Jr. wrote to his friends in New York and laid out in detail what he thought was happening. Since Calhoun would never abide the use of military force against his state, Wright said, he would accept some kind of "arrangement" with Clay to block Jackson's exercise of the Force Bill. The Verplanck bill would be jettisoned, whereupon Clay would step forward with a "peace offering" in the form of a substitute tariff, which Calhoun would immediately pronounce "an acceptable offering to S. Carolina." Then the Clay and Calhoun forces would "join to put down the war bill as they call it." Thus these two men would claim credit for preventing bloodshed and preserving the Union.[34]

It did not quite work out as Wright predicted, but it came fairly close. What he failed to grasp was the fact that Clay was also in consultation with northern congressmen, especially the pro-tariff senators who, like Webster, rejected his seven-year compromise plan. He kept telling them that he had not abandoned his commitment to protectionism—at least not permanently—and that the seven years gave manufacturers an enormous economic advantage. Besides, it would prevent war—and war would benefit no one. Compromise involved sacrifice, and they must decide whether the Union was worth the price.

Clay held two meetings with the protectionist senators. Webster attended the first, but he had to be summoned for the second. Unfortunately, Clay got nowhere. The protectionists told him there was insufficient inducement for them to vote for his plan. He would have to come up with something more enticing. John Tyler may have thought time was "of little importance," but it was important to the protectionists, so Clay set about reworking his plan to win over these northern senators. What he finally devised was a scheme in which the seven-year truce would be stretched out to nine and a half years. During this period only minuscule reduction of the rates would be permitted. Not until July 1, 1842, would there be a sharp drop, and rates would then be lowered to a uniform 20 percent ad valorem. After 1842, duties would be levied in accordance with the needs of the government "until otherwise directed by law."[35]

Clay brought the plan to his northern colleagues and appealed to them for their support for the sake of the Union, and they finally capitulated, promising to vote for the scheme. He then approached the southern congressmen, who readily agreed to the new plan as well, since the principle, not time, was their main concern. Calhoun eagerly gave his consent, for the agreement would allow South Carolina to emerge from the confrontation with honor.

Clay now had his compromise—and it was real. Both sides had gained what they wanted, and both had sacrificed something.

On February 12, 1833, Clay rose in the Senate and presented his plan. It was founded, he said, on "that great principle of compromise and concession which lies at the bottom of our institutions." It was true, he declared, "that my friends do not get all they could wish for; and the gentlemen of the other side do not obtain all they might desire; but both will gain all that in my humble opinion is proper to be given in the present condition of the country."[36]

No sooner did Clay finish his speech than Calhoun jumped to his feet and announced that he approved the principles of the bill and would support it. The reaction in the chamber was instantaneous. The gallery roared its approval, and the senators joined in the applause. In that moment everyone knew that the crisis had passed, bloodshed had been avoided, and the Union saved.[37]

Since all revenue bills must originate in the House of Representatives, according to the Constitution, Clay got his fellow Kentuckian Robert Letcher to move to strike the Verplanck bill and substitute Clay's Senate bill. This action came so suddenly that Jackson's supporters were caught off guard, and the substitute bill "swept like a hurricane" through the House.[38] On February 26, it passed by a vote of 119 to 85. Then, on March 1, the Senate approved it 29 to 16. The Force Bill also passed, and on March 2, a Saturday, the president signed both, starting with the Force Bill. Then he signed the Compromise Tariff of 1833 and it became law.[39]

South Carolina promptly repealed its Ordinance of Nullification but then nullified the Force Bill. But it was a feeble gesture of defiance, and Clay said it should be laughed at and not treated seriously. All anyone could think of was that the Union had been saved, thanks to the Great Compromiser. Clay said it was "the most proud and triumphant day" of his life.[40]

True, a compromise had been achieved—but the problem of slavery that underlay the issue still remained. "The tariff was only the pretext," Jackson insisted, "and disunion and a southern confederacy the real object." Then he predicted what would happen sooner or later: "The next pretext will be the negro or slavery question."[41]

The nullification controversy of 1832–1833 brought the nation within a hair's breadth of civil war. Both sides were armed; both determined to achieve their goals. Although the tariff had been the motivating factor, slavery was the hidden fear that had produced the conflict. And that fear lingered long after the tariff ceased to be debated.

During the Jacksonian years economic issues provided the political dynamite that produced sectional explosions. Over the next few years, however, those issues slowly evaporated and were replaced by a scramble for territory and the implementation of a new ideology called "Manifest Destiny." With Manifest Destiny came a renewed sectional conflict and a battle to control the spread of slavery.

In a sense, Manifest Destiny began with Andrew Jackson. He had a dream of empire—and he expressed it many times. In a letter he wrote to General James Winchester just prior to the War of 1812, he said that with "less than two million [dollars we] can conquer not only the Floridas but all Spanish North America."

All Spanish North America! He helped realize that dream in part by seizing Florida from Spain in 1818, when he was sent by President James Monroe to subdue the Seminole Indians along the southern border. The secretary of state, John Quincy Adams, arranged the treaty by which Spain not only sold Florida to the United States but also relinquished its claims to the Pacific Northwest.

Westward expansion was exactly what Jackson believed was essential for the safety of the nation. With a few thousand volunteers, he continued in his letter to Winchester, "I think [we] could look into Santa Fe and Mexico—give freedom and commerce to those provinces and establish peace, and a permanent barrier against the inroads and attacks of foreign powers on our interior—which will be the case so long as Spain holds that large country on our borders." It was dangerous, he declared, "to leave a foreign power in possession of heads of our leading branches of the great mississippi." Expansion was "necessary for the security of the great emporium of the west, Neworleans." Besides, he went on, "the god of the universe had intended this great valley to one nation." And that nation—obviously—was the United States.[42]

The expansion continued in 1845 with the acquisition of Texas. Mexico had freed itself from Spanish rule and encouraged Americans to settle into its northern border with the United States. Many slave-owning southerners from Alabama, Mississippi, and Tennessee took advantage of the opportunity and expected to be annexed by the United States in short order. This desire turned to determination when Mexico abolished slavery. In 1836, Texas proclaimed its independence, and an army led by Sam Houston defeated a Mexican army at San Jacinto led by the president of the Mexican Republic, General Antonio López de Santa Anna.

In 1845, President John Tyler arranged a joint resolution of both houses of Congress approving the admission of Texas into the Union as a slave state. The annexation bill was passed and signed on March 1, 1845, just a few days before the new president, James Knox Polk, took office. Polk, a Jackson protégé, had narrowly defeated Henry Clay in the presidential election of 1844 on a platform that made expansion its top priority. Indeed, the campaign slogan, "Fifty-Four Forty or Fight," called for nothing less than the "reoccupation" of the entire Pacific Northwest, an area that at the time both the United States and Great Britain jointly occupied. Now the United States wanted all of it, right up to the 54°40' parallel, the border of Russian Alaska.

This idea of American expansion was summed up in an essay written in 1845 by John L. O'Sullivan, editor of the *Democratic Review*, in which he argued that American claims for western territory was "by the right of our manifest destiny to overspread and to possess the whole of the continent which Providence has given us for the development of the great experiment of liberty and federative self government entrusted to us."[43]

Manifest Destiny!—a continent given us by Providence to further our experiment of liberty and self-government. Quite a presumption. But President Polk was not nearly as interested in Oregon as he was in California, with its splendid ports along the Pacific Ocean and the promise of future trade with the Orient. So he readily agreed to a treaty with Great Britain on June 15, 1846, that drew a line between the United States and Canada in the Northwest at the 49th parallel. In his quest for California, Polk offered to purchase it from Mexico, and when he was refused he decided that force would be necessary to demonstrate America's commitment to Manifest Destiny.

The president ordered General Zachary Taylor to advance with his troops stationed near the Nueces River to the Rio Grande, an area considered to be a kind of "no man's land" between the two countries. This action virtually guaranteed an attack by Mexico. And it came on April 25, 1846, when a detachment of Mexican soldiers crossed the Rio Grande, ambushed an American scouting party, and killed sixteen soldiers. When word of this action reached Washington, Polk immediately informed Congress that Mexico had invaded the United States and "shed American blood on American soil." Both houses immediately recognized that a state of war existed between the two countries, a declaration that Polk signed on May 13.

During the relatively short war that followed, which brought repeated military victories to the United States, slavery immediately became an integral issue. Representative David Wilmot of Pennsylvania offered an amendment to an appropriations bill on August 8, 1846, known as the Wilmot Proviso, stating that "as an express and fundamental condition to the acquisition of any territory from the Republic of Mexico . . . neither slavery nor involuntary servitude shall ever exist in any part of said territory." Wilmot assured his colleagues that he did not oppose slavery where it already existed, such as in Texas, but free territory, such as the area that most likely would be obtained from Mexico, involved a different situation. "God forbid," he cried, "that we should be the means of planting this institution upon it."[44]

Southerners instantly shouted their protest when Wilmot completed his presentation. They expected to expand their "peculiar institution" into whatever area was acquired from Mexico without having to contend with such nonsense as the Pennsylvania Representative proposed. Nevertheless, northerners quickly added their support to the Wilmot Proviso, and it passed the lower chamber only to suffer defeat in the Senate, where southerners had greater voting strength.

Each year of the war, the amendment was introduced, and each year it won approval in the lower house and defeat in the upper. Southerners denied that Congress had the authority to forbid the expansion of slavery, claiming that slaves were property and property was protected under the Constitution. For northerners to insist upon such a right threatened the continuation of the Union, they argued. Equally determined were northern abolitionists, who decried the return of the "peculiar institution" to any area that had been free of slavery under Mexican law.

"As if by magic," reported the *Boston Whig* of August 15, 1846, the Wilmot Proviso "brought to a head the great question which is about to divide the American people."

The war with Mexico lasted less than two years. Following the defeat of a larger army of Mexicans at Buena Vista in February 1847 by a force led by General Zachary Taylor, and the capture of Mexico City on September 14, 1847, by American troops commanded by General Winfield Scott, President Polk dispatched Nicholas Trist of the State Department to hammer out a treaty with Mexico to end the war. Trist succeeded in negotiating the Treaty of Guadalupe Hidalgo on February 2, 1848, by which the United States acquired California and New Mexico as well as the "no man's land" north of the Rio Grande. In return, Mexico received $15 million plus assumed claims of $3.25 million of U.S. citizens against Mexico. The territories acquired by this treaty had been free of slavery under Mexican rule and were now regarded by southerners as available for the expansion of their "peculiar institution."

The sectional discord between the North and the South intensified still further after the treaty with Mexico was signed and ratified. Southerners demanded access to a portion of the territories that had been acquired in order to expand their particular culture, including slavery. Northerners, naturally, were vehemently opposed.

Not surprisingly, the issue was caught up in the presidential election of 1848. The Democrats nominated Lewis Cass for president. Former territorial governor of Michigan and a member of Jackson's cabinet, Cass supported popular sovereignty, or squatters' sovereignty, which argued that the question of slavery should be left to the local government in the territory rather than Congress. But another party emerged, the Free Soil Party, consisting of dissident Democrats and members of the Liberty Party. Free Soilers favored the Wilmot Proviso, and their platform called for "free soil, free speech, free labor and free men." They nominated former president Martin Van Buren. Once again Henry Clay sought to head the Whig ticket, but the convention decided to try another successful general and chose Zachary Taylor instead. The general eked out a narrow victory, winning 163 electoral votes to Cass's 127. Van Buren did not receive any electoral votes but took enough popular votes away from Cass to give Taylor the election.

But the question remained: Would slavery be introduced into the new territories? Members of Congress from the North and the South returned to Washington in 1848 spoiling for a fight over the issue. By the time General Taylor assumed the presidency on March 4, 1849, the nation verged on a sectional crisis of catastrophic proportions. Once again, the nation was headed toward disunion and possible civil war.

2

THE CRISIS AND THE RETURN OF THE GREAT PACIFICATOR

Again, war loomed. And the threat was real. As the fear of conflict grew following the war with Mexico, the thoughts of many Americans turned once again to Henry Clay, the man who had rescued the country twice before. But he was no longer in Congress. He had left the Senate in 1842 and made an unsuccessful bid for the presidential nomination of the Whig Party in 1848. Defeated and heartsick, he retired to his home, Ashland, in Kentucky, to tend his livestock, try to forget politics, and improve his health.

When friends and former colleagues urged Clay to imitate John Quincy Adams and return to Congress, he waved them aside. "I do not think," he wrote, "that Mr. Adams added anything to his fame, by his services in Congress after his retirement from the Presidency."[1] But Clay was wrong. As a member of Congress in the mid-1840s, Adams had led the fight against the "gag resolution," a rule that prohibited antislavery petitions in Congress, and this had certainly added to his legacy, if not his fame. The ordeal over the series of gag rules ended in a triumphant reaffirmation of the right of citizens to petition their government for redress of grievances.

In any event, the Kentuckian rejected the call to again serve his country. Although he felt he had done a sufficient job in congress, he did allow for a possible change of heart. "If I could be persuaded that I could materially contribute to the proper adjustment of the momentous question which has grown out of the acquisition of New Mexico and California," he said, "I should cease to feel any repugnance to the resumption of a seat in the Senate."[2]

Clay repeated these sentiments to a number of friends. Nevertheless, as the crisis intensified, it became increasingly clear that the Kentucky legislature was determined to elect him to the Senate despite his protestations, especially since the Free Soil question would most likely be acted on by the next Congress. Clay himself soon began to reconcile himself to the inevitable. In a letter to Thomas B. Stevenson in January 1849, which Clay wrote from New Orleans, a favorite vacation spot, he obviously knew what the legislature planned to do. "I suppose that I shall be elected to the Senate by the General Assembly of Ky, in which case I shall hardly feel myself at liberty to decline, confered as the office will be without any solicitation from me, *without* my being a candidate, and with the knowledge of my strong disinclination to return to that body." Then he cited the reasons for which he had decided to acquiesce to the will of the legislature. First, he said, he was impelled by his sense of "deference to the

will of the General Assembly," and then by his "*sense* of duty,"
and finally by the fact that he might be able "to do some good"
and settle the problem of the expansion of slavery so that secession and civil war would be averted.[3]

On his way down to New Orleans, Clay had run into the
president-elect, General Zachary Taylor, aboard the steamship
Princess at the Baton Rouge landing. This meeting had come
about when the general passed Clay's dinner table, recognized
the diner, bowed, and continued on his way. Taylor was not a
particularly imposing individual, except on a horse. He was
muscular, broad shouldered, had a long nose, prominent cheek-
bones, and deeply lined cheeks.[4] Clay had no idea who the man
bowing to him was, but another gentleman whispered to him:
"Mr. Clay, that is General Taylor."

"It is?" declared the much-surprised Clay. And with that he
rose from his chair, swiftly pursued the general into the adjacent
hall, and extended his hand.

"Why, General," Clay blurted, "you have grown out of my
recollection!"

Taylor grasped Clay's hand and shook it vigorously. "You
can never grow out of mine," came the gracious response.[5] And
with that the two men parted. But it was a convivial beginning for an association that would soon develop into a touchy
relationship.

Indeed, there were many men in the Kentucky General Assembly who feared that if the members elected Clay to the Senate he would use his position to embarrass and humiliate the
new administration out of revenge for having lost the Whig
presidential nomination. However, a number of prominent

Kentuckians, including Robert P. Letcher and John J. Crittenden, assured the legislature that Clay would provide Taylor with
his wholehearted support. That endorsement made a difference.
Besides, most Kentuckians felt that Clay had earned this final
tribute in recognition of his outstanding services over many
decades to the state and nation. So the General Assembly, by a
vote of 92 to 45, elected Clay to the U.S. Senate over Democrat Richard M. Johnson in February 1849. The Great Compromiser was informed of this election in a letter from John
Sloane. "I rejoice at your election to the Senate of the United
States," wrote Sloane, "and most heartily congratulate you on
the occasion. . . . In these days of inordinate personal ambition
it is cheering to see that there is one State in the union where attachment to the honor and interest of the nation prevails over
all personal considerations."[6]

Clay harbored mixed feelings about his election, and he let
out a long sigh. "I really had no wish to return to the Senate,"
he told Joseph R. Underwood, "and shall go back with some
thing like the feelings which the day laborer may be supposed to
have, who having worked hard all day by sun shine, is sent again
into the field to work by moon light." Then, with a smile, he
added, "I do not however apprehend any danger from lunacy."[7]

Despite his national acclaim, Clay knew there were many
Kentuckians who resented his attempt to prod the state into
emancipating their slaves. There was a large number of property owners who needed slaves to work their hemp plantations,
and Clay's continuous calls to outlaw the institution infuriated
them. What precipitated the public acknowledgment of his position was the request of several abolitionists for a statement

from him that they could use to influence the delegates to a convention to be held in the fall for the purpose of amending Kentucky's constitution.

Clay had long argued for gradual emancipation and insisted that his opinion had never changed. Ironically, he owned slaves himself, and would continue to do so, although for many years he had advocated the slow emigration of blacks to some "colony" outside the United States, such as Liberia in Africa. He felt that "color, passions, and prejudices would forever prevent the two races from living together in a state of mutual union." Slaves born after 1855 or 1860, he said, should be freed upon reaching the age of twenty-five; those born before that date would remain in bondage until they died. He did not care which date was chosen so long as a day "be permanently fixed, from which we could look forward, with confidence, to the final termination of slavery within the limits of the Commonwealth."[8]

And why should Kentucky slaveholders agree to his plan? The reasons, he said, could be summed up in a few words. First, because there would no longer be a "servile" race of black men and women, and they could then reach out to enjoy the blessings of liberty and social equality provided in this country. Second, it would "elevate" the character and social condition of the white laborer. Lastly, it would attract capital to Kentucky and improve agriculture throughout the state.[9]

Despite the opposition in Kentucky to his opinions, and with the acquisition of California and New Mexico and the question of their admission into the Union becoming a matter of public debate, Clay decided to publish his opinions on the issue in the local press. It took the form of a letter and was first published in the *Frankfort Commonwealth* and the *Lexington Observer and Kentucky Reporter*, in early March 1849, and then republished throughout the country. His statement boldly reaffirmed his support for the "gradual and ultimate extinction" of slavery in Kentucky. Nevertheless, despite his reputation and appeal, the convention chose to disregard his call for gradual emancipation.

Many praised Clay for his courage. The *New York Daily Tribune* of March 10 disagreed with Clay's proposal of a gradual emancipation but applauded his efforts to end the "peculiar institution" in Kentucky. The *Cincinnati Daily Atlas* of March 5 hailed his statement and called it "strictly an Antislavery document." And former governor of Illinois, Edward Coles, sent Clay a letter written by Thomas Jefferson that he thought would help him in his effort to bring about gradual emancipation in Kentucky. In the letter, written in 1814, Jefferson stated that the "love of justice and the love of country plead equally the cause of these people [slaves]." He further declared it "a moral reproach" that no serious effort had been made to end slavery. Clay thanked Coles for the letter but feared that "the prospect is not very encouraging of adopting any plan at present in Kentucky," due to the agitation by abolitionists in the North and the rivalry between Whigs and Democrats, each of whom feared "that the other would obtain some advantage, if it espoused the cause of Emancipation."[10]

Not everyone appreciated Clay's letter: Abolitionists as well as slaveowners tore into it with a vengeance. William Lloyd Garrison, for example, had read the statement for gradual emancipation in the hope of finding Clay "less selfish, less inhuman, less cowardly" than he had been in past public speeches, especially the "detestable" one he gave in the Senate on February 7, 1839. "But I see no evidence of this in your epistle," he wrote to Clay. "Nay . . . it is remorseless in purpose, cruel in spirit, delusive in expectation, sophistical in reasoning, tyrannous in principle."[11]

Slaveowners also took exception to Clay's call for gradual emancipation. Slavery was so fundamental to their culture, their way of life, and their livelihood that any proposal for emancipation in whatever form infuriated them. And such a proposal, coming from a slaveowner such as Clay, made it that much worse. By the late 1840s southerners no longer made excuses for the fact that their lives depended on slavery. Now they argued the benefits of the institution for both whites and blacks, comparing the lives of slaves favorably to those of white laborers toiling in northern factories.

Clay had been warned that the letter could do him infinite harm throughout the country and undercut his national support, especially in Kentucky. But these warnings did not deter him in the least. "As I regret to hear that [it is] not popular, I suppose that my letter will bring on me some od[ium]," he wrote. "I nevertheless wish it published. I owe that to the cause, and [to] myself, and to posterity."[12]

———

Clay decided to spend the summer of 1849 in the East to improve his health. He had a dreadful and incessant cough and felt perpetually tired. He hoped that a visit to Saratoga and

Newport would help. At the moment, he said, "I am somewhat reduced in flesh, and debilitated in strength, altho my health is otherwise good. I trust that the mineral water [in Saratoga], followed by the Sea bath [in Newport] will restore me."[13]

And, not surprisingly, what this northeast tour produced was an outpouring of affection from a great number of Americans, who sought him out to tell him how much they loved and admired him. Indeed, Henry Clay was probably the most popular man in the country now that Andrew Jackson was dead—and he knew it. He told his friend Christopher Hughes that he was surrounded by "a constant stream of visitors."[14] Wherever he went, large numbers of people appeared, waving to him, screaming his name, and hoping he would respond. The mobs "pester him to death," reported Philip Hone of New York, "haunt him by day, serenade him by night, follow him in his walks, shouting, hurrahing, Henry Claying him wherever he goes." On arriving in Syracuse, Clay "went through some trying scenes" when a mob pursued him. Said Clay: "To escape the overwhelming crowd, I sought an asylum, and, for more than half an hour, was locked up . . . at the Globe Hotel, the multitude thundering all the time to get in."[15]

Clearly Henry Clay was indeed the most popular man in the United States[16]—unless he ran for president. Then his past would catch up with him—especially the charge that he had prevented Jackson's election as president in 1825 and supported John Quincy Adams. In the fall election of 1824 there had been four candidates for the presidency—Andrew Jackson, John Quincy Adams, William H. Crawford, and Henry Clay—none of whom won a majority in the Electoral College. So the election went to the House of Representatives as required by the Constitution. When Clay, then Speaker of the House, threw his support behind Adams, thereby winning him the election, the friends of Old Hickory publicly claimed that Clay had entered a "corrupt bargain" with Adams by offering his support to the New Englander for president in return for appointment as secretary of state. At that time the office of secretary of state led straight to the White House.[17] To the day he died, Clay swore he had not made a bargain with Adams. The only thing he regretted, he later admitted, was that he had accepted the post of secretary of state from Adams, a move that "injured both him and myself,"[18] a move that also tended to validate the "corrupt bargain" charge by Jacksonians.

Henry Clay's lack of discipline also helps to explain why he never won the presidency. Unlike Daniel Webster, he did not take the time to polish his speeches before publication so as to sharpen his arguments, make them more compelling, and win popular approval. Instead he spent countless hours carousing, gambling, drinking, and flirting with attractive women. What is tragic about Clay was that he could have been a better politician, lawyer, statesman, husband, father, and friend if he had made up his mind to do so—even though he was indeed a remarkable and outstanding American statesman.

Margaret Bayard Smith, wife of Senator Samuel Harrison Smith of Maryland, claimed that Henry Clay had greater intellectual strength than any man she had ever met, and that included Thomas Jefferson and James Madison. Those two former presidents had a far better education than Clay, coupled with more "favorable circumstances" in their lives. "Not so Mr.

Clay," Margaret Bayard Smith wrote. "Whatever he is, is all his own, inherent power, bestowed by nature and not derivative from cultivation or fortune. He has an elasticity and buoyancy of spirit, that no pressure of external circumstances, can confine, or keep down. . . . He is a very great man."[19]

—————

Clay enjoyed the "seabath" at Newport but once back home in Kentucky he came to the conclusion that he was now too old, too tired, and too worn out to experience any real joy in the demonstrations of public recognition. Still, he appreciated the fact that the people understood and applauded his many services to them. Above all, he was dedicated to preserving the Union, and now he must return to the Senate and do what he could to keep the country whole. For that ordeal he felt he must rest up and regain his strength.

He knew he faced slave owners who were determined to introduce their "peculiar institution" into California and New Mexico. "No one can be more opposed than I to the extension of slavery into those new territories," he wrote. He hoped that when Congress reconvened in December a spirit of calmness and candor would prevail. After all, as fellow citizens of such a "glorious country," we must "exercise mutual and friendly forbearance."[20]

Unfortunately, recent elections in northern states in 1848 gave little hope for calmness and friendly forbearance. Whigs had suffered heavy losses in Ohio and Pennsylvania, which would make it more difficult for Clay to find the majorities he needed to attempt any compromise. In early November, he finally decided to leave his home in Kentucky and visit friends in New York and Philadelphia before heading for Washington. These friends might help him with ideas about how to proceed. It was a leisurely trip, and he told each crowd that gathered along the way that he understood the "great, threatening and alarming questions" facing the country. He said he did not believe slavery would be introduced into California and New Mexico because of the climate and character of the country and its inhabitants. And he wanted his listeners to know that he stood pledged "under all circumstances and in all storms TO STAND BY THE UNION." He assured them that he would do everything in his power to prevent "the dissolution of the Union . . . and all the horrors of civil war."[21]

As he headed south from New York and Philadelphia to Washington he was startled to find at the Baltimore depot an enormous crowd that had gathered, he said, "without preconcert or arrangement." Here was a crowd in, of all unlikely places, a railroad station. That was surprising. These people had come not only to salute him and show their affection and support, but also to impress upon him their need and hope that he would use his considerable gifts to find a solution to the gathering crisis facing the country. When he tried to escape, they followed his carriage from the depot to his hotel in town, cheering him, waving to him, and calling his name. They did not relent when he entered the hotel. When he appeared at an open window on the second floor, they slowly quieted in the hope that he would speak to them. A few of them called out, "Speak to us!" Clay shook his head. "We are too far apart, my friends, to do that," he shouted to them. But he went on to say that he would meet with them the next day and shake each person by the hand.[22]

And he kept his word. At 11 a.m. Clay positioned himself between two parlors on the first floor of the Barnum City Hotel and received the throng. First he told them how delighted he was with the reception he had received, and then he met each person individually. Most members of the crowd left the hotel feeling reassured that Clay would bring sanity and a sense of calm to Washington and find the means to appease both North and South, thereby ending the crisis.[23]

When Clay finally reached Washington, he checked in at the National Hotel. Again crowds pursued him. Each day they came to his hotel, repeating the pleas he had heard throughout his trip. Benjamin Brown French, former clerk of the House of Representatives and a keen reporter of the Washington scene, marveled at what was happening. "It seems to me," he wrote, "as if he [Clay] was 'the observed of all observers' instead of the President." At the White House the Great Compromiser was surrounded as he passed through the East Room. "I could not but think," French continued, "that, after all, he was the idol of the occasion. 'Henry Clay' is a political war cry that will at any time and in any part of this Union create more sensation among men of all parties than any other name that can be uttered. . . . He now stands, at the age of three score years & ten, the beau ideal of a patriot, a statesman, a great man!"[24]

That phrase, "beau ideal," was repeatedly used by others at the time. A young representative from Illinois, Abraham Lincoln, who had just completed his first term in Congress but had not sought reelection, said that Henry Clay was "my beau ideal of a statesman, the man for whom I fought all my humble life."[25]

But Clay's arrival in Washington and the adulation accorded him everywhere aroused the jealousy and concern of the administration. President Taylor's aides believed that Clay intended to assume control of the Whig Party and act out the role of leader of the nation. And that belief did not bode well for a close relationship between the president and the Great Compromiser.

———

On Monday, December 3, 1849, Clay appeared in the Senate for the opening of the thirty-first Congress. It was quite a moment. His arrival created a sensation. Other senators rushed to his side to greet him, and a thunderous ovation ricocheted around the chamber. He was overcome by the emotions expressed on his return to Congress. "Much deference and consideration are shown me by even political opponents," Clay commented with a sense of pride. "I shall by a course of calmness, moderation and dignity endeavor to preserve these kindly feelings."[26]

But as Clay took his seat, he looked old and worn. He coughed a good deal, and his cheeks were shrunken. Still, his wide mouth was "wreathed in genial smiles," just as in years past. He was back where he belonged, and not much had changed during his absence. At the age of nearly seventy-three, he "generally kissed the prettiest girls wherever he went," enjoyed a game of cards in his room, and downed a large glass of bourbon whenever he relaxed.[27]

As he looked around the chamber, Clay recognized many old friends and enemies, men who had played a major role during the Jacksonian years and still exercised considerable influence in national affairs. There were Thomas Hart Benton of Missouri, Willie P. Mangum of North Carolina, Lewis Cass of Michigan, John M. Berrien of Georgia, and, of course, the other two members of the Great Triumvirate, Daniel Webster and John C. Calhoun.

But there were also new members who, through their intelligence and leadership would shape national affairs for the remainder of the coming decade. These included Jefferson Davis of Mississippi, Stephen A. Douglas of Illinois, Salmon P. Chase of Ohio, John Hale of New Hampshire, Jeremiah Clemens of Alabama, and William H. Seward of New York, among others.

But the more he surveyed the scene and contemplated the heavy burden of the expectations placed upon him, the more Henry Clay worried. "Upon the whole," he told Mary S. Bayard, a Philadelphia friend, "there is a very uncomfortable state of things here both for the Whig party, and I fear for the Country. From both parties, or rather from individuals of both parties, strong expressions are made to me of hopes that I may be able to calm the raging elements. I wish I could, but fear I cannot, realize their hopes."[28]

It would take great statesmanship to calm the raging elements. To many, that included the end of slavery. But Clay himself was not optimistic that the abolition of slavery could be achieved in the near future—at least not without a struggle. "I confess," he wrote to Robert S. Hamilton, "that I have not much hope that Slavery will ever be extinguished in any of the States, by legal enactment, at least for a long time to come." Why? There were three reasons, he said: first, the "violent and indiscreet course of Ultra abolitionists in the North"; second, the "great amount of property invested in Slaves"; and third, the "repugnance with which a People change long established habits."[29]

Clay's worries intensified as he studied the membership of Congress. The Whigs had done poorly in the last election, and now they numbered 105 in the House of Representatives, compared to 112 Democrats. There were 13 Free Soilers, and they held the balance of power. More than half of all these congressmen were freshmen. Of the 34-member New York delegation, for example, 22 were first-termers. And they were young: The average age was forty-three, and only two members of the House were over sixty-two. Worse, most of these freshmen were hotheads, and that guaranteed trouble.[30]

Democrats controlled the Senate as well as the House with a margin of ten votes. To make matters worse, the Whig Party started to break apart. On December 1, two days before the congressional session began, the House Whigs held a caucus in which they expected to choose their candidate for Speaker. The southern members were led by two Georgians: Robert Toombs, "the stormy petrel, often grand as a declaimer, and always intolerant, dogmatic and extreme"; and Alexander H. Stephens, a sickly looking firebrand of "fragile frame, and delicate sensibilities."[31] During the preliminary debate in the caucus they used all their considerable skills to get the northern Whigs to agree not to impose the Wilmot Proviso on California or New Mexico or to attempt to terminate the slave trade in the District of Columbia. But they failed in their efforts. When the northern Whigs refused their appeal, Toombs, Stephens, and most of the southern Whigs walked out of the caucus, swearing they would block any northern Whig from a position of leadership in the House or the party unless he first promised to repudiate the Wilmot Proviso.

Those Whigs who remained in the caucus—almost exclusively northerners—enthusiastically voted to support Robert Winthrop, a Massachusetts Whig, for the position of Speaker of the House. A scholarly Boston patrician, he was much respected because of the excellence of his service as Speaker in the previous Congress. But without southern votes his election seemed hopeless.

Trouble flared as soon as the House assembled. As expected, the fight began over the selection of the Speaker, since that officer would appoint all the committees and thereby control the legislative agenda. The contest involved eleven candidates, and the balloting turned long and ugly and exhausting. In addition, the question of slavery in the territories loomed ever larger as members rose to nominate or support a particular candidate. At one point in the proceedings, Toombs became so overcome with emotion that he threatened dire action. "I . . . avow before this House and country," he ranted, "and in the presence of the living God, that if by your legislation you seek to drive us from the territories of California and New Mexico . . . and to abolish slavery in the District of Columbia, thereby attempting to fix a national degradation upon the States of this Confederacy, *I am for disunion* and . . . I will devote all I am and all I have on earth to its consummation."[32]

The House broke out with angry shouts. The presiding clerk, Thomas Jefferson Campbell, tried to keep order but failed. Members kept up a noisy response, and some sneered their contempt, having heard these threats many times before. But Alexander H. Stephens leapt to his feet and reiterated what Toombs had said: "I tell this House that every word uttered by my colleague meets my hearty response. . . . I would rather that the southern country should perish . . . than submit for one instant to degradation."[33]

After the nominations, when the members finally got around to actually voting for Speaker, the Democrat, Howell Cobb of Georgia, received 103 votes, while the Whig, Winthrop, obtained 96, but because there were scattered votes for other candidates, mostly by Free Soilers, neither Cobb nor Winthrop had the necessary majority to win. So the House proceeded to a second, a third, and a fourth ballot—all without success. One day followed the next, one week followed another, as the representatives tried to work their way out of the impasse. Each night the Whigs caucused and reaffirmed their commitment to Winthrop. At the same time the southerners refused to vote for him unless he repudiated the Wilmot Proviso.

Day and night the members shouted at one another. And at one point a fistfight broke out that degenerated into a melee. "Had a bomb exploded in the hall," reported the sergeant-at-arms, Nathan Sargent, "there could not have been greater excitement."[34]

Dueling challengers became commonplace. Many northerners sneeringly rejected them out of hand. For someone like William Yancey of Alabama, however, "most daring of the firebrands in the 1840s, 'a duel was only a pleasant morning recreation.'"[35]

By the time the House reached the forty-first ballot, at least thirty candidates had been put forward for election. Still no one had won a majority of votes. Finally, on the fifty-ninth futile attempt to name a Speaker, Frederick P. Stanton of Tennessee suggested on Saturday, December 22, 1849, that if the members continued to fail to decide on their leader after three more attempts, the House would agree to allow the person who had won a plurality of votes to become the Speaker.

That had never happened before, but the weary members readily agreed. On the sixty-third ballot, Howell Cobb received 102 votes to Winthrop's 99, and he was declared the new Speaker. But what had happened in the election of the Speaker was repeated in deciding other House officers—though at a faster pace. It took only twenty ballots to name the clerk, fourteen to choose the doorkeeper, eight for the sergeant-at-arms, and three for the chaplain. All told, it had taken three weeks for the House to organize itself.

———

If the situation in Washington was bad, the situation in the southern states appeared ominous. For the past several years John C. Calhoun had been urging southern unity as a means of counteracting northern aggression. In a speech given in the Senate in 1849, he demanded that a southern convention be called in order to bring about the unity necessary to protect southern interests. "I have, Senators, believed from the first," he declared, "that the agitation of the subject of slavery would, if not prevented by some timely and effective measure, end in disunion." It would not happen quickly as the result of a single blow, he said: "Disunion must be the work of time." The Union could be saved if the North would "do justice by conceding to the South an equal right to the acquired territory." The South needed "justice, simple justice," and could offer no compromise except the Constitution. It would offer "no concession or surrender."[36]

This call for a convention stirred a response from a number of southern leaders. The governor of Virginia, for example, told his legislature that if the Wilmot Proviso passed Congress, "then indeed the day of compromise will have passed, and the dissolution of our great and glorious Union will become necessary and inevitable." Other southern legislatures, such as Florida and North Carolina, responded favorably to Calhoun's summons for a convention, and meetings were held in Alabama, Tennessee, and Georgia to give delegates a chance to express their desire for unity and resistance. Quite obviously, a southern movement to promote that unity had begun.[37]

A convention, such as Calhoun had proposed, would certainly have helped to bring southern states together, but to have South Carolina send out a call would have been unwise in view of that state's involvement in the nullification controversy. If South Carolina had "attempted to lead" in the crisis, said one, it would be ruinous to the cause; instead, South Carolina should be kept "*out of sight*" as much as possible.[38]

So Mississippi stepped in to undertake the task. A convention held in that state on October 1, 1849, passed a resolution that included a statement avowing devotion to the Union. But it went on to condemn the idea that Congress had the right to prohibit slavery in the territories, abolish slavery in the District of Columbia, or agitate for the emancipation of slaves. The time had arrived, read the resolution, when the South should come together and decide on what action to take. The resolution further stated that a convention of the slaveholding states should be held at Nashville, Tennessee, on the first Monday in June, next, to devise and adopt some method of resistance to northern aggression.[39] Several months later, the Mississippi state legislature added its endorsement for convening the Nashville meeting. The call quickly gained approval from all the southern states, and the most extreme of those who eventually attended the convention planned to initiate secession.[40]

——

As the situation deteriorated and the southern states prepared to attend the Nashville Convention, Henry Clay realized that he had to do something quickly to head off what seemed like a certain catastrophe. First, he decided he had to help generate a public outcry against disunion, especially in the border states, so he wrote to several leaders in Kentucky and pleaded for their assistance. "The feeling for disunion, among some intemperate Southern politicians," he explained to Leslie Combs, "is stronger than I supposed it could be." The masses of people of the South were yet sound, he continued, but they might become inflamed by agitators. The best remedy for such a situation was "popular expressions at public meetings of the people," and such meetings should be held throughout Kentucky. "Can't you get up a large, powerful meeting of both parties" at Lexington, Louisville, and other cities "to express in strong language their determination to stand by the Union," he asked Combs. To help in the effort, he included in his letter a series of resolutions that he would "be happy to see adopted." These resolutions included the following:

1. Resolved, That this meeting is firmly attached to the union of these States, and that they go for it, one and indivisible, now and forever.
2. Resolved, That whilst this meeting would be most happy that the controverted question of slavery within the Territory recently acquired from Mexico, should be settled in a manner satisfactory to all parts of the Union, no settlement of it, whatever it may be, will create any just occasion for dissolving the Union.
3. Resolved, That the meeting beholds, in the dissolution of our glorious Union, no remedy for any alleged evils, real or imaginary, but a great aggravation of them all, and contemplate that deplorable event as the parent of other calamities, far transcending in magnitude and fatal consequences any of which complaint is now made.
4. Resolved, That, as far as depends on us, we will stand by, support, and uphold the Union against all attacks from without or within, and against all ultraism, whether at the North or the South.[41]

Numerous meetings were indeed organized and held throughout Kentucky, and resolutions very similar to those suggested by the senator were passed.[42] Meanwhile, Clay told his son that he had "been thinking much of proposing some comprehensive scheme of settling amicably the whole question [of slavery in the territory acquired from Mexico], in all its bearings but I have not yet positively determined to do so." Unfortunately, he said, "some of the Hotspurs of the South are openly declaring themselves for a dissolution of the Union, if the Wilmot Proviso is adopted." "This sentiment of disunion," he added, was more alarming than he had feared.[43]

———

The situation became more urgent and complicated when workmen building a mill for John Sutter, a Swiss immigrant, discovered gold in the foothills of the Sierra Nevada in the Sacramento Valley of California. Despite Sutter's efforts to keep the discovery secret, news of it spread rapidly, and prospectors from all parts of the United States rushed to the gold fields to find the metal. California was suddenly flooded with people who crossed the plains by wagon, fought their way through the jungles of Panama, or sailed around the tip of South America at Cape Horn. These forty-niners, as they were called, were northerners for the most part, and California suddenly became a pulsating area whose population zoomed from 6,000 to 85,000 virtually overnight.

With this new development, President Taylor immediately saw a possible solution to the overall problem of slavery in the territories, so he sent a confident Congressman T. Butler King of Georgia, a Whig, to California as his special agent to urge the people to hold a convention, write a constitution, and apply for admission as a state in the Union, bypassing the usual period of territorial status. Taylor thought he could avert disunion by submitting a plan to Congress, asking that they do nothing until California came forward with a request for statehood together with a completed and ratified constitution. Immediately thereafter, New Mexico would also apply for admission.

What made Taylor's plan unworkable at the very outset was the fact that, when the delegates met in California to write their constitution, they specifically excluded slavery. They wished to be admitted as a free state. And since New Mexico was free of slavery under Mexican rule, it too would likely ask for admission as a free state, something southern congressmen had no intention of allowing, given their commanding military role in acquiring this territory in the Mexican War.

There were other problems with Taylor's plan. For one thing, it did not take into account the fact that Texas claimed a large portion of New Mexico, including Santa Fe. Any attempt at admitting New Mexico necessarily involved Texas, which Taylor simply ignored. If a boundary was to be drawn, how would it be done, and who would do it? In addition, the boundary question was tied up with a debt problem. Texas had a debt of more than $11 million resulting from the loss of revenue from customs at its ports of entry, as a consequence of annexation, and therefore held the United States partially responsible for the debt. New Mexico led to Texas which led to the debt. How would each segment of this problem be resolved? Taylor ignored the debt question as well and simply asked Congress to admit New Mexico as a state.

Further complicating the matter was the presence of Mormons in Utah. As members of Joseph Smith's Church of Jesus Christ of Latter-day Saints, who had been led to the Great Salt Lake in Utah by Smith's successor, Brigham Young, the Mormons had drafted a constitution for the creation of a provisional state called Deseret and also planned to apply for admission into the Union. Inasmuch as Deseret did not permit slavery, and was not involved in a land dispute with Texas, its admission into the Union should have been uneventful—except that many leaders of the Mormon religion at that time practiced polygamy. That fact alone had enough controversial firepower to prevent admission for the foreseeable future.[44] But there it was: Three western territories were asking for admission, and all of them— California, New Mexico, and Deseret—would become free states. Southerners would never agree to such an outcome without sufficient recompense.

Southern Whigs were reluctant to quarrel with the administration, but they had no intention of standing by while the territorial gains of the Mexican War were denied them. Not a few demanded an extension of the 36°30' line to the Pacific Ocean with slavery permitted south of that line, including California. Others argued for a tougher fugitive slave law so that slave owners would receive greater assistance in recovering runaways. Any number of northern states had laws prohibiting officials from involvement in recapturing runaways, laws that southerners claimed violated the Constitution. Accordingly, Senator James M. Mason of Virginia proposed on the Senate floor during the first week of 1850 a new fugitive slave bill that was much stronger than the previous law, which had been passed in 1793.

And northern Free Soilers had demands as well. They insisted that Congress terminate both the slave trade and the institution of slavery in the District of Columbia. It was embarrassing and humiliating for the nation to have foreigners come to a supposedly free, democratic, civilized and Christian country and see human beings bought and sold on the auction block in the capital city. Both practices had to end. But if they did, responded southerners, secession would ensue. As Toombs so dramatically said on the House floor, "abolish slavery in the District" and "*I am for disunion.*"[45]

So by 1850 these several sets of demands—a number of which stood in direct opposition to one another—threatened to explode into secession and civil war. Only a compromise satisfactory to both sides could prevent this catastrophe. Fortunately, there sat on the floor of the Senate a statesman who would find the means of concocting such a solution, a political genius of the first rank.

3

A Possible Solution

As Henry Clay knew all too well, the nation had already begun to fall apart. Five years earlier, the Methodist and Baptist churches had split, North and South, over the question of slavery, and this profoundly worried the Great Compromiser. If Christian churches could not remain unified in addressing the problem, could the nation itself mend its divisions? Or was it doomed to failure?

Even Daniel Webster, who tended to downplay the slavery quarrel, was astounded by what he saw and heard upon arriving in Washington for the start of the congressional session. "There is so much excitement & inflammation on the subject of Slavery, Dissolution, &," he exclaimed, "as that it overwhelms, or threatens to overwhelm, all really important measures." Nonetheless, he made light of it: "All this agitation, I think, will subside, without serious result, but still it is mischievous, and creates hurt burnings. But the Union is not in danger." Things would "cool off," he predicted. It was just a matter of time. He said he would remain silent during the expected debates on the subject in the Senate, but if something dire developed, then "I shall have something to say."[1] Indeed.

John C. Calhoun, the third member of the Great Triumvirate, returned to the Senate looking beaten and desperately ill. He had about him the specter of death. Feeble to the point where he needed vocal assistance in order to address his colleagues, he was fighting to stay alive so he could serve (however weakly) in the defense of his beloved South. There were several other senators in the chamber who, like Calhoun, had fought many of the battles of the Jacksonian era and now seemed ready to depart from active participation in the affairs of Congress—men such as Thomas Hart Benton of Missouri and Lewis Cass of Michigan. They were old, and they no longer dreamed and plotted to win the presidency. The new generation—William H. Seward, Salmon P. Chase, John P. Hale, Stephen A. Douglas, Jefferson Davis, and Jeremiah Clemens—had begun to take over control of Congress. Their voices and deeds would dominate the decade of the 1850s as each tried in his own way to avert a bloody civil war.

Some of these new men, such as Douglas, did not regard slavery as a moral issue. Rather, in their minds, the issue was purely political, something the people had a right to decide for themselves through the ballot box. For these men, popular sovereignty was the only democratic way to resolve the problem—an idea that Calhoun, Davis, and Clemens regarded as sheer nonsense.

This situation, and the fact that the administration could not come up with a viable plan which could get through Congress, compelled Clay to give serious thought to working out his own scheme. If he succeeded, he could reassume control of the Whig Party, now that he was back in Washington and ready to take charge of the nation's affairs. The party had rejected him in 1848 as its candidate for the presidency. Now the Whigs would learn again how much they needed Henry Clay if they were to survive as a functioning political organization. The president's plan called on Congress to do nothing until California and New Mexico formally applied for admission into the Union; Henry Clay now felt he could provide something more substantial. Undoubtedly, his pride, in large measure, convinced him that he must sit down and work out a compromise that each side could accept, as impossible as that might seem.[2]

But more than mere pride motivated Clay. Genuine patriotism stirred him to lay everything else aside and devote all his energies to finding the road to peace and reconciliation. And he was not prompted by any hope of gaining the White House. He had once sought the presidency with a desperation that had led him to foolishly accept the office of secretary of state from President John Quincy Adams, a decision that had produced the "corrupt bargain" charge. In 1850 he was no longer driven by this once-obsessive dream. Physically he was worn out. He coughed incessantly, complaining of colds, but more likely he suffered from the onset of tuberculosis. "We have so far had a bad winter here," he wrote his wife in January 1850, "and I have had my customary colds but they have not been as bad as I have had, nor laid me up."[3]

Another thing. He was old. At the age of seventy-three he no longer felt he could appeal to the American electorate for the right to serve them as president of the United States. Instead, as Daniel Webster later noted, Henry Clay felt the overwhelming desire "to accomplish something for the good of the country during the little time he had left upon earth."[4]

As Clay set about trying to produce a solution that would address all the issues involved in the crisis, he was overcome by conflicting emotions: at one moment, the fear that nothing could be proposed that would satisfy both sides, and at the next, the exhilarating sense and hope that he must and could find the solution. "Slavery here is the all engrossing theme," he wrote in January 1850 to James Harlan, one of his most loyal supporters in Kentucky: "My hopes and my fears alternately prevail as to any satisfactory settlement of the vexed question. . . . I shall not however offer any scheme unless it meets my entire concurrence."[5]

Clay informed both family and friends that he was working diligently on his proposal, but that he knew time was slipping by very rapidly. In Congress, events took an alarming direction almost immediately. First off, early in the congressional session, Senator Henry Foote of Mississippi introduced a bill for the organization of the two territories acquired from Mexico; then Mason proposed a tougher fugitive slave law; and now in mid-January 1850, Senator Benton produced a Texas boundary bill. Those rapid movements in the Senate caused Clay to speed up his own efforts, since not one of these other plans constituted a compromise. Each one served separate northern or southern interests.

Still, he was not at all sure that he could come up with a proposal that would be able to neutralize the crisis, and this made him very nervous. Exacerbating his anxiety was the knowledge that he would not have the support of the administration in any proposal he put forward. For the past several months since arriving in Washington and meeting with the president and members of his cabinet, Clay had made it clear in every letter he wrote to his political friends and to members of his family that although his relations with the administration were cordial, they were not confidential. The administration did not trust his motives. And with good reason. They were certain he was maneuvering to win back the leadership of the Whig Party.

Nor did the administration seem any more cordial toward him by the time he was ready to put forward his scheme in late January. He told Boyd McNairy, a close friend, that his "relations to the present Administration are not hostile," but he had "no reason to feel that it has any particular disposition to oblige me."[6] What Clay was about to propose would not find favor in the White House. He was on his own.

Clay was one of the few men in Congress who understood that any proposal would have to address each one of the several issues raised since the conclusion of the Mexican War, starting with the status of California and New Mexico and including the Texas boundary and debt, slavery and the slave trade in the District of Columbia, and a new fugitive slave law. Throughout the early weeks of January 1850, he worked out all the details for a "comprehensive plan" so as to produce a compromise agreeable to both the North and the South. To achieve this, he later said, "I . . . cut myself off from the usual enjoyments of social life" in order to "restore the blessings of concord, harmony and peace."[7]

By January 21 Clay had a complete scheme in mind. But before presenting it to the Senate he decided he needed the active support of Daniel Webster for the proposals. He felt that Webster's Second Reply in the Webster-Hayne debate provided proof that the Massachusetts senator could find the language and emotion to achieve a compromise that would save the Union. Clay decided therefore to visit Webster at his home and ask for his assistance.

It was a miserable evening. Except when invited to important dinner parties, Clay rarely went out at night because of his weakened physical condition and hacking cough. It was a rainy night and the Great Compromiser showed up unannounced at Webster's residence at 7 p.m. looking "very feeble." Although the two men belonged to the same party, they had not been close, and at times had verged on an open rupture. At best, their relationship could be described as "formal." The pity is that they could have been very helpful to each other had they not been competitors for the same high office. All the Clay Whigs, commented John J. Crittenden, a leading Kentucky Whig, "desired to see Clay and Webster elected to the Presidency, and we felt that to accomplish this object it was necessary that Mr. Clay should come first, but we were never able to make Webster and his personal friends see this, and therefore neither of them won the prize."[8]

Both men were outstanding statesmen. Both should have occupied the White House. But neither of them was able to inspire confidence in the American people. Neither man was trusted.

And in this democratic age they were both misfits. They really belonged with generations that had gone by. Sadly, the electorate seemed to know this. As the former Democratic senator from Illinois Sidney Breese said to Webster, "How unfortunate for the Country that you adopted opinions adverse to the democracy! Had you not, you would have been President."[9]

The same could be said about Clay. The "corrupt bargain" charge against him when he helped to elect Adams over Jackson in 1825 ruined any chance he might ever have had to gain the presidency. But that was all in the past. Now Clay could think only about saving the Union—and he needed Webster's help. The eloquent voice of the Massachusetts senator, combined with the political genius of the Great Compromiser, would surely rescue the nation from its present crisis. That was Clay's hope and desire. That, too, was the prayer of many Americans.

The two men faced each other on that rainy night and reached an important understanding. Webster noticed that his visitor looked haggard and coughed incessantly. They spoke for an hour, Clay outlining what he intended to propose in the Senate to effect a compromise between the warring factions, and Webster interrupting at times with questions and suggestions. As he listened, Webster "thought Mr. Clay's objects were great and highly patriotic. . . . That perhaps Providence had designed the return of Mr. Clay to the Senate, to afford the means and the way of averting a great evil from the country." Webster also thought that Clay's plan would be "satisfactory to the North, and to the reasonable men of the South." Still he did not commit himself, not until he had a chance to study the individual proposals in depth. But he assured his former rival that he would be supportive and said he agreed in substance to what Clay had proposed.[10]

Clay emerged from Webster's home completely exhausted, but he was invigorated by a sense of accomplishment. Two members of the Great Triumvirate would stand together and fight for the preservation of the Union. As for Calhoun, the third member, he had long indicated his belief that secession was inevitable if the South was to protect its rights and way of life.

Clay spoke to no other northerner about his scheme—or so he said—but he did consult with several southerners because he knew it would be harder to convince them that the Union must be safeguarded at all costs. He was very careful about the number of men with whom he discussed his proposals. He kept the number small. As he admitted a month later on the floor of the Senate, he had learned a lesson back in 1833: "I consulted too many," he admitted, "the effect of which was to endanger the fate" of the Compromise Tariff of 1833.[11] He would not repeat that mistake.

———

Finally, on January 29, 1850, Henry Clay decided his proposals were ready for presentation to the full Senate and the American people. He could wait no longer. He must stop refining them. He must start the process of achieving compromise. It was Tuesday, and when the Senate convened, Clay rose and addressed the chair.

"Mr. President," he called out in a still strong and vibrant voice, "I hold in my hand a series of resolutions which I desire to submit to the consideration of this body. Taken together, in combination," he continued, "they propose an amicable arrangement of all questions in controversy between the free and slave States, growing out of the subject of slavery."

He paused momentarily. Then he said he hoped that the care and deliberation he had devoted to the preparation of "this great national scheme of compromise and harmony" would be considered by each senator "before he pronounces against the proposition embraced in these resolutions."[12]

The package contained eight resolutions. The first provided for the admission of California to the Union without the imposition by Congress of any restriction in respect to the exclusion or introduction of slavery within its borders. The second resolution was like the first. Since slavery did not exist by law in New Mexico, and was not likely to be introduced into that territory, Congress should not attempt to introduce or restrict it there but instead should leave the decision to the people of the territory. Popular sovereignty would determine the issue. Clay believed that the Mexican law forbidding slavery still applied, something southern extremists emphatically rejected. Besides, they argued, settlers in the territories could not decide the slavery question until the territory formally applied for admission into the Union as a state. Prior to that application, slave property was protected by the Constitution and could be taken at any time into the territory.

The third and fourth resolutions, Clay said, should be considered together because they were closely connected. The third called for the settlement of the Texas boundary, and the fourth for the assumption by the United States of Texas's debt acquired before annexation, on condition that Texas formally relinquish to the United States any claims which it had to any part of New Mexico. The amount of the debt to be paid, however, was not specified. Clay did not think it was asking too much of Texas to make this commitment for the sake of bringing peace and harmony to the country.

As for the boundary of Texas, Clay felt it should extend from the mouth of the Rio Grande to the southern limits of New Mexico, and then to the line, established by Spain and the United States in the Treaty of 1819, by which Florida had been acquired.[13]

The Great Pacificator also linked the fifth and sixth resolutions. The fifth declared that it was "inexpedient" to abolish slavery in the District of Columbia while it still existed in Maryland, from which the District had been carved. The sixth stated that it was "expedient" to prohibit the slave trade within the District. No slave could be sold as merchandise, Clay declared, or be transported to other markets outside the District. He said that he wanted to stop the slave trader from coming to the District to establish his jails and marching his slaves through the avenue leading from the Capitol to the White House.

The seventh resolution called for a more effective fugitive slave law, a problem so evident, Clay said, that he did not wish to comment further at that time. Later he would discuss it at length. The eighth and final resolution declared that Congress would have no power to prohibit or obstruct the trade in slaves among the slaveholding states and that such matters fell exclusively within the laws of the particular states involved in the trade.[14]

Here was compromise. Here was a plan with something for each side. Here was a possible solution to the problems the nation faced. Under Clay's plan, North and South would each gain something it desired, but in exchange each would have to make a sacrifice.

At this time Clay offered no extended speech in support of the proposals. He wanted the other senators to have the opportunity to study his scheme and perhaps improve on it. He therefore asked that his proposals be made the order of the day for the following Tuesday.

Meanwhile, for the remainder of the week, Clay not only worked on the speech he would give in support of his scheme but also contacted friends and allies in various sections to the country and begged them to help generate popular enthusiasm for his proposals: "I shall need, therefore, popular support," he wrote to one ally. "Large public meetings (one at New York especially), indorsing my plan substantially, would do much good." He further suggested that a good time to initiate this support would be after his upcoming speech the next week or the week following. But these meetings must not appear to have been directed by Congress or any other outside organization. They must appear to be a spontaneous local demonstration of public feeling. "Its beneficial effects will depend much upon its being conducted and regarded as a local and spontaneous assemblage, without any ground for the imputation of its being prompted from any exterior source."[15]

As he had requested, a week later, on Tuesday, February 5, Clay rose again to defend his proposals and plead with other senators to join him with their support. This was to be his major effort, and he needed all the strength he could muster. Upon arrival at the Capitol, Clay asked a colleague for a helping arm to get him up the stairs and into the Senate chamber. As he entered the room he looked ready for battle. "Erect, calm and serene," he carried about him the dignity the occasion demanded.[16]

It was 1:00 p.m. when he began his address to his colleagues, and he spoke straight through for two and a half hours—which was usually as long as he could speak without losing his voice. It was a heroic effort.

"Never," Clay began, "on any former occasion, have I risen under feelings of such deep solicitude. . . . I have never before risen to address any assembly so oppressed, so appalled, so anxious." Then he turned to the presiding officer and continued. "And, sir, I hope I will not be out of place to do here what again and again I have done in my private chambers—to implore of Him . . . to calm the violence and rage of party—to still passion—to allow reason once more to resume its empire."

There could be no mistake, he declared, that it was party passion that had brought them to this wretched state, and it must be stilled. Nothing was more damaging to the country at large than party passion. Nothing was more corrosive, nothing more destructive. It was hateful. Then, he felt compelled to assure his audience that he spoke out of concern for the preservation of his country and not out of any ambition for a higher office. That desire had finally faded. Now his sole purpose in life was to bring the country together to prevent the likelihood of secession and civil war.

He paused and then began a long explanation and defense of his compromise. Regarding the first resolution, the admission of California, the people of that territory, he reminded his listeners, had already decided the question. And had it not been the doctrine of all parties that when a state was about to enter the Union it had the right to decide the question of slavery? Thus, those who had argued for the application of the Wilmot Proviso must realize that as soon as any territory entered the Union as a state, the proviso would cease.

Score one for the North in winning another free state, and score one for the South in omitting all mention of the Wilmot Proviso.

Regarding the second resolution, popular sovereignty, Clay appealed to his northern colleagues who wished to apply the proviso to territory obtained from the Mexican War to recognize that by law slavery did not exist in New Mexico and most likely never would. Think and recognize the fact, he said, that "you have got what is worth more than a thousand Wilmot provisos." Nature was on their side. Why try to improve on it? The proviso was not needed to get what they wanted, and in fact could bring only harm. He then begged them to "elevate" themselves "from the mud and mire of mere party contentions" and act "as responsible men, and as lovers of liberty, and lovers, above all, of this Union."

Again, both sides could claim a victory.

Regarding the third and fourth resolutions, Clay insisted that there was not a single resolution in his entire proposal that did not contain some "mutual concession, or evidence of mutual forbearance." The people of Santa Fe strongly opposed any union with Texas, Clay said, and therefore he hoped that the boundary of Texas could be settled through mutual agreement without having to appeal to the Supreme Court. These were questions that were not proper for the high court to decide; instead, they were "great political, national, and territorial questions, which transcend their limits, and to which they are utterly incompetent." As far as Clay was concerned, the present boundaries of Texas were proper and just, and the assumption of her debt of not less than $3 million, was the discharge of an obligation by the United States for the loss of Texas's right to collect duties when she was an independent nation.

Here was a clear instance of mutual concessions.

At this point Clay ended his speech and the Senate adjourned for the day. It was understood that Clay would resume his argument the following day, February 6. He needed a rest, and he needed to remain silent for a few hours to recover his voice.

The next day Clay started off by concluding his remarks on the Texas question and then moved to the fifth resolution. He insisted that Congress had the right to legislate about slavery in the District of Columbia because it governed the District. Such power, he said, existed "here, or it is nowhere." And if the institution of slavery existed in Maryland, then Congress, "in conscience and good faith," could not abolish it in the District, inasmuch as the District had been ceded to the government by the state of Maryland back in 1791. Nevertheless, he insisted, the people of the District ought to have a say in deciding whether slavery should or should not exist in their community. Otherwise, the government of the United States, with respect to the people of the District, was "a tyranny, an absolute Government." For a people to live in a condition that violated the "great principle which lies at the bottom of our own free institutions" was unacceptable.

Clay then explained the "mutual concessions" that each side in the controversy would sustain. The fifth and sixth resolutions asked both North and South to put aside their respective prejudices. Clay claimed that the fifth resolution, about slavery in the District, conceded "all that the South . . . ought in reason to demand." As for the slave trade in the District, he called it "repugnant," the elimination of which both sides should "rejoice to adopt."

Regarding the seventh resolution, the extremely controversial fugitive slave law, Clay said that every state and the officers of every state—indeed, "every *man* in the Union"—had the "obligation to assist in the recovery of a fugitive slave . . . who escapes into one of the free States." This was not a concession by the North, he argued. This was a constitutional obligation. Property was protected under the Constitution, and slaves were property. When an owner of a slave asserted his rights to regain possession of his property, "every man present," said Clay, was "bound to assist in the execution of the laws of their country."

At one time, twenty or thirty years ago, Clay continued, the North had laws that helped a slave owner recover his property. No more. Now there were laws to obstruct the recovery of runaway slaves. Therefore Congress must see to it that a stronger fugitive slave law was enacted as "enjoined by the Constitution." It was only right, and that was why it was part of the compromise.

The final resolution, Clay hoped, would "forever" put an end to the question of whether Congress did or did not have the power to regulate the slave trade among the slaveholding states. It was based on a principle that he was sure both sides would acknowledge and agree to.

In sum, Clay presented these resolutions as "an olive branch to both parts of this distracted, and, at this moment, unhappy country." He concluded his presentation by assuring the members of the upper house that he was more than willing to surrender any part of his proposal in favor of something better. He appealed to the South to pay no mind to those who argued for the extension of the Missouri Compromise line to the Pacific Ocean. By demanding that slavery be permitted south of 36°30', they would as a consequence admit the fact that slavery would be prohibited north of that line. Such action would affirm the right of Congress to legislate about slavery in the territories. Was that what they wanted? he asked. "Non-action by Congress is best for the South," he said, "and best for all the views which the South have disclosed to us."

Clay closed his speech with an emotional outburst. "Here I stand," he declared, within the Union, "and here I mean to stand and die." Make no mistake, the Constitution was made for "posterity, undefined, unlimited, permanent and perpetual." He implored both northerners and southerners, "by all their love of liberty—by all their veneration for their ancestors—by all their regard for posterity . . . to pause—solemnly to pause—at the edge of the precipice, before the fearful and disastrous leap is taken into the yawning abyss below." Should secession occur, "I pray I may not survive to behold the sad and heart-rending spectacle."[17]

———

When he finished, northerners and southerners thought long and hard about what they would gain and what sacrifices they would be required to make in return. The North would have a free California and New Mexico and an end to the slave trade in the District of Columbia. But they would have to accept a tougher fugitive slave law. The South would obtain a better fugitive slave law, the continuation of slavery in the District, and no mention of the Wilmot Proviso. But it would have to give up California and New Mexico and the possibility of ex-tending the Missouri Compromise line to the Pacific Ocean. As Clay had said, the compromise involved mutual concessions.

It seems clear from his two speeches that Clay's main appeal was directed toward northern senators, since he believed they would have to make the greater concession, especially in ap-proving a tougher fugitive slave law. Yet when he first proposed his eight resolutions on January 29, the first eight senators to rise with objections were southerners, and all but one were Dem-ocrats. They disliked the Texas boundary, and the debt question, and the idea of compromise. They sneered at the very idea of compromise as a solution to the crisis. But, as Clay might have expected, when he concluded his remarks on February 6, both sides complained that their side received little and the other side received everything.

When Clay finished his marathon address, he was totally drained. Over the past two days he had spoken for nearly four and three-quarter hours. As he wrote to his wife on February 7, the effort had exhausted him, but he expected to recover his strength in a few days. Whether his efforts would have the desired effect remained to be seen, he added, "but all agree that my movement and Speeches have done good."[18]

———

Although various parts of his scheme had come from other congressmen, Clay's important contribution was his plan of bringing all the issues together and treating them not as a single bill but as a single problem. To find a solution required that all parts of his proposal had to be accepted so that each side would be satisfied. That was the heart of compromise. And, of course, he tried to balance the gains and losses of both sections so that they could consent to the whole. The exclusion of the slave trade in the District was another one of Clay's contributions to the package.

The public reaction to Clay's speech was very favorable, including many previous rivals and adversaries. For example, President Martin Van Buren, one of Andrew Jackson's closest advisers, wrote to Francis P. Blair, the former editor of the *Washington Globe*, the mouthpiece of the Democratic party, and asked Blair to do him a favor. "Tell Clay for me," Van Buren wrote, "that he added a crowning grace to his public life . . . more honorable & durable than his election to the Presidency could possibly have been."[19] Van Buren's sentiments summed up the thinking of most Americans. Blair sent the letter to Clay with one of his own and watched as the Kentucky senator absorbed the contents. After reading both letters, Clay rose from his chair, walked over to Blair, and extended his hand. It was a new age.

"Henry Clay," editorialized the *New York Herald*, "may never reap the reward of his devotion to the United States, to the Union, and to the constitution, but posterity will do him justice, if the present generation do not."[20]

"In five hundred years to come," argued the *Frankfort Commonwealth*, "it is not probable that an opportunity will occur to elevate his equal. Greece produced but one Demosthenes, Rome but one Cicero, and America, we fear, will never see another Clay."[21]

There were naysayers, of course. Edward Everett of Massachusetts said, "I do not think much of Clay's compromise as a whole"; and William H. Seward of New York termed it a "magnificent humbug." Senator Chase called the compromise "sentiment for the north . . . and substance for the south—just like the Missouri Compromise."[22]

Four days later, on Sunday, February 10, 1850, an unexpected ally in the cause of saving the Union called on Clay at his hotel. It was Thomas Ritchie, the leader of the Richmond Junto (a political machine) and editor of the *Richmond Enquirer* back in the Jackson days. Ritchie wholeheartedly approved of Clay's efforts and had come to wipe away years of disagreement be-tween them in the cause of rescuing the Union. Thereafter, Ritchie argued at length in the *Washington Union* for Clay's compromise proposals.

———

During the next six months, Clay worked diligently to stir up popular support for his compromise, and he instructed his friends to organize general meetings of local citizens to express their favorable opinion. And almost immediately, such meetings were held. A gathering of several thousand people from all par-ties congregated at the Castle Gardens in New York on Febru-ary 25, and they endorsed Clay's compromise plan and pledged their undying allegiance to the Union.[23] Slowly it became ap-parent that the American people throughout the country—not just those in the East—were awakening to the danger of dis-union and registering their concern. Each time Clay received notices of the resolutions passed at public meetings that de-manded action by Congress in arranging a compromise, he pre-sented them in the Senate and added his voice to their concern about the need for an immediate resolution of the crisis. "Nine-teen twentieths, if not ninety-nine out of a hundred people of the United States," he insisted, "desire most anxiously a settle-ment of the question . . . and the restoration once more of peace, and harmony, and fraternity."[24]

Perhaps most important of all in advancing his compromise, Clay, starting in early February, summoned a daily caucus of both Whigs and Democrats who were committed to preserving the Union. As chairman of the group, he guided, advised, and encouraged them in their efforts to work out a compromise. One thing the caucus clearly achieved was the universal realization that this was not a partisan effort. Both parties demonstrated their will to achieve a solution to the problem. In managing this highly diverse group of individuals, Clay operated through Lewis Cass when he wanted to address conservative Democrats and Stephen A. Douglas when he wished to contact more liberal-minded Democrats. He later admitted that he spent more time "in conference and consultation" with Democrats about his compromise than he did with Whigs.[25]

—

Debate on Clay's resolutions began in the Senate on February 11 and continued until March 27. Meanwhile, the House of Representatives heard a series of orations by the friends and followers of John C. Calhoun. Needless to say, they were critical of any plan that did not capitulate totally to their demands.

In February there were twenty-two formal speeches in the House, nine delivered by southern Democrats, four by southern Whigs, three by northern Democrats, five by northern Whigs, and one by a northern Free Soiler.[26] Albert C. Brown of Mississippi and Samuel W. Inge of Alabama were the most vociferous defenders of southern rights; they not only listed the grievances of their section but studded their speeches with threats about what would happen if these grievances were not addressed. They were answered by men such as Thaddeus Stevens of Pennsylvania and Horace Mann of Massachusetts,

both sharp-tongued orators who could match whatever grievances and threats were thrown at them by southerners. The
most formidable supporters of compromise came from mid-
western Democrats and southern Whigs, but even they insisted
on stipulations that extremists termed unacceptable.[27]

In the Senate the most immediate and vocal opponents to
challenge Clay's plan were John M. Berrien of Georgia and Jefferson Davis of Mississippi. Berrien insisted on the right of
southerners to take their slaves into the newly acquired territories: "If you seriously believe that slavery is a stain upon the
land where it exists," he declared, "—that it will pollute the
soil—that you cannot dwell among slaveholders—if this is your
real belief, then make a partition of the country" and allow
southerners to live in their own portion of the land and enjoy
their way of life. Though he loved the Union, he said, he had a
prior loyalty to his state.[28]

Jefferson Davis accused Clay of surrendering southern rights
in the hope of attracting northern support for his presidential
ambitions. He denied that the North was giving up more than
it would receive in the compromise. It was the South that was
expected to yield its position of equal status in the Union, and
that, he cried, would never be acceptable. As a possible solution
to the problem he seemed to advocate the extension of the Missouri Compromise line to the Pacific Ocean, but he did not ex-
plicitly say so. He kept his options open.[29]

———

On February 11, 1850, the day debate began in the Senate on Clay's proposals, a most important meeting took place in the National Hotel, initiated by the former governor of South Carolina, General James Hamilton. This meeting consisted of a large number of investors and speculators who held securities that included Texas bonds, which would be redeemed at full value if the United States paid the Texas debt. Hamilton was the agent and attorney for owners of over half the debt. What the group decided to do was form a lobby to persuade Congress to assume the Texas debt, thereby enriching the bondholders. It was an ever-modern scheme of greed to favor the propertied few. The lobby, as it developed, worked diligently over the next several months, and their efforts paid off. Hamilton later boasted that "no man in or out of Congress . . . contributed more to the adjustment of [the] Texas question at Washington than myself."[30]

Still another meeting took place in Speaker Howell Cobb's residence on Third Street, when seven members of the House agreed to a plan sponsored by Senator Douglas to be introduced on the floor of the House by Douglas's ally John A. McClernand of Illinois. According to this plan, bills would be introduced by which New Mexico and Utah (the area Mormons called Deseret) would be made territories on the basis of popular sovereignty; California would be admitted as a free state; and slavery would be continued in the District of Columbia. These bills would be interconnected. Of the seven members who attended the meeting, two were southern Whigs, Alexander H. Stephens and Robert Toombs, and the fact that they were willing to assist the passage of a Democratic plan indicated the growing willingness of congressmen of both major parties to reach a compromise that would save the Union.[31]

At one point, James D. Doty of Wisconsin, a Free Soiler, introduced a scheme in the House that California be unhitched from the other measures and admitted as a free state—a very popular proposal. But such a proposal guaranteed the failure of any compromise, since it was the interconnectedness of the many issues at stake that provided the surest route to success. Speaker Cobb and his allies worked feverishly to kill Doty's suggestion. Thirty roll calls in quick succession took place, and the debate went on until after midnight. Exhausted but determined, a majority succeeded in finally forcing an adjournment and the House approved it without the members acting on California's admission. The leadership saw to it that in the following days there was enough business on hand to prevent a repeat of Doty's scheme. It was a close call.[32]

In the upper house, Senator Benton rose to express his opposition to Clay's package. Ever the Jacksonian, he had tangled many times with the Great Pacificator. Now in 1850 he prepared to tangle once again with his opponent. He argued against Clay's proposals and against a compromise in general. Making California part of a system of measures to settle the slavery question in the United States was not the way to go, he argued. California deserved to be considered separately: "I am opposed to this mixing of subjects which have no affinities," he said. Mixing it all up in "the nature of a compact or compromise" was wrong and simply would not work.[33]

Clay responded immediately. "There are, no doubt, many men who are very wise in their own estimation," he taunted his opponent, "who will reject all propositions of compromise, but that is no reason why a compromise should not be attempted to be made. I go for honorable compromise whenever it can be made. Life itself is but a compromise between death and life, the struggle continuing throughout our whole existence, until the Great Destroyer finally triumphs. All legislation, all government, all society, is formed upon the principle of mutual concession, politeness, comity, courtesy; upon these, everything is based."[34]

———

One of the major obstacles to a compromise was the fact that President Taylor had offered a plan in his special message to Congress that his allies felt was the best way to avoid conflict and possible disunion, namely, to leave the resolution of the problem to the executive. After all, Taylor was a military officer and would certainly know better than a collection of quarreling members of Congress how to handle conflict, if it occurred. The president actually told any number of visitors to the White House that he would personally lead whatever military force was necessary to crush a rebellion. He spoke of levying an embargo and blockading southern ports: "I can save the Union," he assured Horace Mann, "without shedding a drop of blood."[35]

Taylor's proposal for the admission of California as a state should have been referred to the Senate Committee on Territories, but Senator Henry S. Foote of Mississippi suggested that it be submitted instead to a special committee, along with all the other resolutions offered by Clay, and brought forward as a single bill that encompassed everything.

Clay objected. Although his resolutions were intertwined, he never intended that they be joined in a single measure. "I do not think it would be right to confound or to combine all these subjects," he said. Senators, he believed, should have the right to vote for one part of the package but against another. Of course he hoped that all the resolutions would be passed, just as happened with the Missouri Compromise in 1820. But he felt that each resolution should be debated on its own merits.

Foote feigned astonishment. "I am grieved—I am mortified," by this reversal of direction, he protested. The resolutions had been offered to that body, he continued, "to cover the *whole* ground of controversy" as a way of adopting a compromise. Why not put them all into a single bill?

In responding, Clay unfortunately referred to Foote's remarks as a "sort of omnibus speech," invoking the name of the newest form of urban transportation into the congressional lexicon. Later the word "omnibus" referred to the entire compromise and became popularized. Into this omnibus, Clay snickered, Foote had introduced "all sorts of things and every kind of passenger, and myself among them." The gallery broke out in laughter at that remark. "My desire was that the Senate should express its sense upon each of the resolutions. . . . I never did contemplate . . . bringing them all into one measure."

Foote persisted. He also accused Clay of failing in his responsibilities as a native son of the South by giving the North "all the *trump cards* in the pack."

That accusation infuriated Clay, who said, "I know no South, no North, no East, no West to which I owe my allegiance. . . . My allegiance is to this Union, and to my own State."[36]

But President Taylor wanted California detached from the package and debated as a single item—not to be part of an omnibus bill. As the debate grew more intense, the president, both publicly and privately, assured all Americans that he was prepared to save the Constitution and the Union—even if it necessitated the shedding of blood.

With the Nashville Convention looming ahead, the situation had indeed become ominous.

4

THE GREAT TRIUMVIRATE WEIGHS IN

John C. Calhoun was dying. By early March he had very few weeks left to live. Still he was determined to speak his peace about what had to be done to save the Union. He had attended few sessions of the Senate since its return. On March 4, hanging on the arm of General Hamilton, he arrived in the chamber to deliver his speech. But the effort of climbing the stairs and tottering to his seat was more than he could endure. He did not have the strength to deliver his own speech. Wrapped in a black cloak, and looking feeble and exhausted, he rose at the proper time and asked to have his speech read by his friend Senator James M. Mason of Virginia. The chair then recognized Mason, who read Calhoun's oration with as much emotion as he could muster.

"I have, Senators," Mason began on Calhoun's behalf, "believed from the first that the agitation of the subject of slavery would, if not prevented by some timely and effective measure, end in disunion." He had tried repeatedly, but without success, to call the attention of the two contending parties to adopting some measure "to prevent so great a disaster." The situation had now reached a period in which it could no longer be denied that the Union was in danger." The Senate must now grapple with the "greatest and the gravest question" imaginable: "How can the Union be preserved?"

Mason paused for a moment and then continued. What was the cause of this threatening calamity? Quite simply, "The immediate cause is the almost universal discontent which pervades all the States composing the southern section of the Union." And what was the reason for this discontent? It was the "long-continued agitation of the slave question on the part of the North." When the Constitution was adopted there had been an "equilibrium" between the two sections in the government. It was a "nearly perfect equilibrium." Each section could protect itself against the aggression of the other. But oh how that had changed. Today one section had "the exclusive power to control the Government," leaving the other section without adequate means of protecting itself from the "encroachment and oppression" of the ruling section. Drawing from the census returns of 1790 and 1840, Calhoun compared the growth of the North with that of the South to show how the North had become dominant in "every part of the Government." The resulting increase in the number of northern states and their majority population (which the census of 1850 would further accelerate, he claimed) meant that the balance of power that had existed when the government commenced would be "effectually and ir-retrievably" destroyed.

If this destruction had been the operation of time without the interference of government, then the South would have no reason to complain. But that was not the case. "It was caused by the legislation of this Government." Specifically, the Northwest Ordinance, the Missouri Compromise, and the Oregon Territory Act excluded the South "from 1,238,025 square miles" of territory. He did not include the territory recently acquired by the treaty with Mexico, Calhoun added. As for the California and New Mexico territories, "The North is making the most strenuous efforts to appropriate the whole to herself, by excluding the South from every foot of it." Since independence was first achieved, the steady, unrelenting deprivation of southern rights had been pursued by the national government. "Such is the first and great cause that has destroyed the equilibrium between the two sections in the Government."

Furthermore, the government claimed the right to decide on the extent of its powers and the right to resort to force, if necessary, to sustain whatever power it claimed for itself against all opposition. What limitations could be placed on the national government? Calhoun asked. If none, how could the states protect the powers reserved to them by the Constitution? If such was the case, then the character of the government had been changed from a Federal Republic, as originally conceived by the framers, to a "great, national consolidated Democracy." As a consequence, the North had acquired a hold over every department of the government. What was once a Republic had been converted to a government as absolute as that of the autocracy of Russia "and as despotic in its tendency as any absolute Government that ever existed."

What senators must take into consideration, Calhoun declared, was the fact that two races exist in the South, which constitute the very foundation of her social system. And the North hates it. The more radical people of the North regard the institution of slavery as "an offense against humanity"; the less radical consider it a "blot and stain" on the nation's character. For southerners slavery is an essential bulwark against "poverty, desolation and wretchedness."

There were many cords holding the Union together, Calhoun admitted. It would take more than one blow to sever them all. These cords were spiritual, ecclesiastical, political, and social. The strongest of these were spiritual and ecclesiastical, consisting in the "unity of the great religious denominations, all of which originally embraced the whole Union." But as powerful as these cords had been, they had not been able to resist the corrosive effect of the agitation over slavery. The first cord to snap had been the Methodist Episcopal Church, which was "now arrayed into two hostile bodies" and engaged in litigation over what was formerly their common property. Next, the Baptists broke, and although the Presbyterians had remained intact, some of the strands had given way. Of the four great Protestant denominations, only the Episcopal Church had remained "unbroken and entire."

If the agitation continued, Calhoun warned, the political cord would surely snap, and then there would be nothing left to hold the Union together but "*force*." And force would certainly keep the states connected, but that connection would take on the character of the subjugation of the weaker section to the stronger. Instead of a "union of free, independent, and sovereign States, in one Confederation," as it existed at the beginning of the Republic, it would be a divided country in which the southern portion would be held in bondage and made to behave in accordance with northern wishes.

Could the Union be saved? Calhoun asked his fellow senators, adding: "To which I answer, there is but one way by which it can be, and that is, by adopting such measures as will satisfy the States belonging to the southern section that they can remain in the Union consistently with their honor and their safety." Do that, and discontent would cease. Harmony and good feelings between the two sections would be restored, and fears over disunion would dissolve.

The South asks for justice, simple justice—and will take nothing less. She has already given so much that she has little left to surrender.

Then Calhoun posed another question: Could a solution be found? Absolutely, he said, but not by the weaker section. It must come from the stronger. The North, he insisted, must do several things: It must accede to the South "an equal right to the acquired territory"; it must assist in the recapture of fugitive slaves; and it must amend the Constitution so as to restore to the South the power she once possessed of protecting herself, before the equilibrium between the sections was "destroyed by the action of the Government."[1]

Calhoun thought an appropriate amendment would be easy to concoct. Actually, his idea was so vague it hardly constituted a specific plan or proposal. All he could do was revile the North for having more people emigrate to its area and consequently acquiring more voting strength in Congress to make up a majority.

A short time later, Calhoun's *Discourse on the Constitution* was published, in which he proposed his personal solution to the problem of disunion. He suggested that the Constitution be amended to provide a dual executive, that is, a president for both sections of the country, with each chief executive possessing a legislative veto. That was the best he could offer. But there was little hope that it would be enacted—or even considered.

When Mason finished reading Calhoun's text, friends rushed up to Calhoun and shook his hand and expressed their enthusiasm for his remarks. Then they helped him rise from his chair, leave the chamber, and return to his boardinghouse. Generally speaking, the speech received mixed reviews. James Hammond, former governor of South Caroline, thought it "very patriotic," but a distinguished Maryland Whig said it was "peevish and feeble." On the whole it did not even excite a large majority of southerners. As far as they were concerned, it was "able," but nothing more.[2]

Three days after Mason read Calhoun's oration, Daniel Webster rose in the Senate and delivered his justly famous "Seventh of March speech" on the state of the Union. But the style, mood, and purpose of Webster's speech were far different from those of Calhoun's. Here was a man who truly loved his country—not merely one section of it—and he spoke with a conviction that moved both his colleagues and the entire country.

It had taken Webster several weeks to decide what to do. A number of senators had attempted to bribe him to reject Clay's proposal in favor of President Taylor's. Shortly after Clay introduced his resolutions, Congressman Robert Winthrop of Massachusetts had come to Webster with a message from a group of southern congressmen, led by Edward Stanly of North Carolina, in which they declared that if the Senate adopted President Taylor's plan and not Clay's, these southerners were "prepared to do their best to make him [Webster] the next President" on a "moderate platform." Obviously delighted by the information, Webster assured Winthrop that he had not "pledged himself" to support the Clay resolutions and was thinking the matter over. "In short," he said, "I am substantially with the President, and you can tell Mr. Stanly so."[3] And there the matter rested for the next few weeks.

But as the debate over the resolutions grew more heated and the talk of secession became louder, Webster started having doubts. For one thing, he realized that the southerners were not bluffing about leaving the Union. For another, he knew that his silence was hindering the efforts of Clay and other men who were attempting to ward off the impending catastrophe. Like it or not, a secession crisis existed, and Webster decided he could no longer remain silent.

On February 24, he wrote his son and informed him that he intended to speak his mind. At the moment he was not sure exactly what he would say "to beat down the Northern and the Southern follies, now raging in equal extremes."[4] He was over-burdened with legal cases, he added, especially before the Supreme Court, but he finally decided that he must put every-thing aside and work on his Senate speech. He devoted a full week to the task, and what resulted was one of his greatest ef-forts in Congress.

In preparing his speech, Webster consulted with several friends, without revealing the gist of his talk. He also spent sev-eral hours with Calhoun before that dying man gave his own speech. Calhoun was very candid, informing Webster of what he planned to say, and that information convinced the Massa-chusetts senator all the more that his talk would have to have real emotional power. Calhoun, said Webster, would adopt his usual "dogmatical assertion, & violent denunciation of the North." As for himself, he said, he meant "to make a *Union* Speech, and discharge a clear conscience."[5]

By early March Webster let it be known that he would de-liver a major address, and whether it be "good or bad," he said, "nobody will care a fig about it a month hence" if peace was restored to the country.[6]

As word got out about his approaching performance, every-one naturally hoped it would be another "Second Reply to Hayne." Expectations ran high. That address, wrote Benjamin Silliman, a lawyer and Whig politician, to Webster, "was a turn-ing point in your life." It established his reputation as a great orator: "Your speech this week may be the turning point in the life of this nation." The country seemed to think that Webster's oratorical skill could disperse the threatening storm. "Do it, Mr. Webster, as you can do it," begged one Democrat, "like a bold and gifted Statesman and Patriot. Reconcile the North and South and *preserve the Union*."[7]

General James Hamilton spoke to Calhoun on the day Calhoun's address was read in the Senate. Suppose Webster succeeds in resolving the issue? asked Hamilton. "What shall we of the South do for him?"

"Make him President, Sir," Calhoun responded, "for he will deserve it for that single act. Besides his eloquence, genius, and his great public services Mr Webster possesses many noble qualities. I shall most probably never recover my health but if I do I would not only not allow my name used against him but would regard it as a sacred duty to support him."[8]

On the evening prior to his scheduled speech, Webster met with several advisers and his son, Fletcher, and he kept "questioning and doubting how it would go." He took extensive notes during the meeting and kept worrying about the outcome. There was strong feeling, he said, both in the House and the Senate, to "bring in California," and "it could be done in ten days" because it was very popular in Congress. However, there were those who insisted on a single bill uniting all the measures if compromise was to be achieved.[9] Either way, Webster hoped that his words could make a difference.

Later that evening, Robert Winthrop returned from Boston and went to see Webster. He found him "in the last agonies of preparation." Winthrop explained that the people in Boston did not want to see the Wilmot Proviso pressed so strongly in his speech as to worsen an already grave situation. Webster replied: "I have not told a human being what I am going to say tomorrow," but said he had no intention of even mentioning the proviso.[10]

The next day, March 7, a mob arrived early at the entrance of the Senate chamber to witness the anticipated oratorical miracle. Every seat was taken. "We have never, we think, on any former occasion," reported the *National Intelligencer* on March 9, "seen the Senate Chamber so crammed with human beings as it was yesterday by the multitudes of both sexes who were attracted thither by an eager desire to hear Mr. Webster's speech." Even the dying Calhoun rose from his sickbed and entered the chamber to hear what his colleague had to say. The tension in the room was almost unbearable.

Finally, the moment arrived. At noon the Senate reconvened, and although Isaac Walker of Wisconsin had the right to conclude his speech of the day before, he appreciated the anticipation that gripped the audience and gallantly yielded the floor to Webster, who was, he said, "the one man, in my opinion, who can assemble such an audience."[11]

Webster rose and thanked Walker. Then he began, and he spoke very slowly. "Mr. President, I wish to speak today, not as a Massachusetts man, not as a northern man, but as an American, and a member of the Senate of the United States. . . . I speak today for the preservation of the Union. 'Hear me for my cause.' I speak today, out of a solicitous and anxious heart."

It was a splendid beginning. It was heartfelt, and everyone in the room knew it.

Webster started off by turning to the subject of the newly acquired territories. At no time, he declared, had he voted to acquire, annex, or cede territory to the North, South, East, or West. "My opinion had been, that we have territory enough, and that we should follow the Spartan maxim, 'Improve, adorn what you have, seek no further.'" With respect to the territories they had just obtained from Mexico, slavery would be excluded; he said, and it would be excluded by a law that should be obvious—"I mean the law of nature—of physical geography—the law of the formation of the earth." In this mountainous terrain, with broken ridges and deep valleys, who would expect to see "a hundred black men cultivating tobacco, corn, cotton, rice, or anything else?" No, sir, California and New Mexico were "destined to be free . . . free by the arrangement of things by the Power above us."

Legally prohibiting slavery in these areas would unnecessarily intensify rancor between the North and the South. But whatever they did, Webster insisted, there must be no evidence or even a hint of reproach to wound the pride "of the gentlemen who belong to the southern States." If a proposition was introduced in the chamber to form a government prohibiting slavery in New Mexico, he said, "I would not vote for it."

As he continued, Webster made it very clear that he blamed both sides for the present crisis. The North and South each harbored many grievances that he would not attempt to discuss in toto. But he did want to address the issue of fugitive slaves, in particular, because he believed that the complaints of southerners had a "just foundation." It had been found that many

northern legislatures and individuals were disinclined "to perform, fully, their constitutional duties, in regard to the return of
persons bound to service, who have escaped into the free
States." In that respect the "South is right," he said, and "the
North is wrong." The South had a just complaint, and it was
well founded. The Constitution, Webster declared, was quite
specific as to the responsibility of individuals and states to return fugitive slaves to their owners. What right did the North
have to attempt to get around the explicit provision of the Constitution? "None at all—none at all." Most probably, because
of the "turmoil of the times," the northern states had not
stopped to consider the obligation that the Constitution imposed
on them. The South had been "injured" and had a right to complain, and the North had been "too careless of what I think the
Constitution peremptorily and emphatically enjoins upon it as
a duty."

Northern Whigs took deep exception to what Webster said.
To ask those who believed that all men were created equal to
participate in the recapture and return of men, women, and children who were seeking freedom was, they said, contemptible,
and they had no intention of acting on Webster's command.

As for northern complaints against the South, Webster declared, it must be remembered that when the Constitution was
adopted, the North recognized the existence of slavery in the
country. But the eagerness of the South to acquire territory and
expand its slaveholding came as a surprise. What had happened
was that instead of slavery being "regarded as an evil," as it
was at the time of the ratification of the Constitution, it was
"now regarded by the South as an institution to be cherished,

and preserved, and extended." Consequently, northerners heard southerners contrast the life of the slave to that of laborers in the North and give preference in every respect to the slaves of the South. Most northerners were farmers and cultivated their own land. They were "freeholders, educated men, independent men." If, on the other hand, they earned wages, they provided "new freeholds, and small capitalists are created." These farmers and wage-earners took offense to have their lives as free men compared with slaves. They did not deserve such mockery. What they had to do throughout the nation, Webster insisted, was "to endeavor to allay the agitation, and cultivate a better feeling and more fraternal sentiments between the South and the North."

Webster also objected to the way free blacks were employed on northern ships as cooks and stewards and were imprisoned when these ships docked at southern ports and kept locked up until the ships departed. This imprisonment was despicable, he said. It was unconstitutional and illegal.

Webster paused as he was about to head into a sensitive topic: secession. He took a deep breath and then began again. "I hear with pain, and anguish, and distress, the word secession," he said, accenting the last word as he spat it out of his mouth. It was especially painful, he thought, when it came from men known all over the world for their patriotism and their public services. "Secession! Peaceable secession! Sir, your eyes and mine are never destined to see that miracle. The dismemberment of this vast country without convulsion!" Who could be so foolish to believe such a notion? "There can be no such thing as a peaceable secession. Peaceable secession is an utter impossibility." Secession would bring war, and he would not describe the horrors that catastrophe would entail. By this time Webster was shouting.

If secession occurred, he continued, "What am I to be?—an American no longer?" What about the flag? Would it remain? Where was the eagle to tower? Was he "to cower, and shrink, and fall to the ground"? If secession occurred, our fathers and grandfathers would "rebuke and reproach" us, and our children and grandchildren would cry out "shame."

Webster declared that he was sorry the idea of secession was ever "thought of, talked of, or dreamed of," in the wildest flights of human imagination. "There will be no secession," he bellowed. "Gentlemen are not serious when they talk of secession." The idea that those who were free could form one government, while those who were slaveholding could form another, was "a moral impossibility."

He said he was ashamed to even speak publicly about splitting the Union. "I dislike it—I have an utter disgust for it, I would rather hear of natural blasts and mildews, war, pestilence, and famine, than to hear gentlemen talk of secession. To break up! To break up this great Government, to dismember this great country! . . . No, sir! no, sir! There will be no secession."

Webster's voice throbbed with emotion. He could barely contain himself. As he continued, he said that instead of talking about these dire things, dwelling in these "caverns of darkness," and grappling with ideas that were "horrid and horrible," they should come into the light of day and revel in the fresh air of "liberty and union." They must not be pygmies when the times call for men. They must make their generation one of the strongest and brightest in that "golden chain" that was destined to bind their people to the Constitution "for ages to come."

Webster then began an impassioned conclusion. "We have a great popular Constitutional Government," he told his colleagues, "guarded by legislation, by law, by judicature, and defended by the whole affections of the people." Who would wish to destroy it? "No monarchical throne presses these States together; no iron chain of despotic power encircles them; they live and stand upon a Government popular in its form, representative in its character, founded on principles of equality, and calculated, we hope, to last forever." Its daily inspiration was liberty and patriotism; its yet youthful history was full of enterprise, courage, and an honorable love of glory and achievement. It had grown in physical size and now extended across an entire continent. Two oceans washed its shores. What more could anyone ask?

In conclusion, Webster quoted from the *Iliad*, conjuring up the image of a shining nation, cleansed by the waters of the Atlantic and the Pacific oceans, and looking as beautiful, as magnificent, and as awe-inspiring as the ornamental border of Achilles' silver buckler:

> *Now, the broad shield complete, the artist crowned*
> *With his last hand, and poured the ocean round;*
> *In living silver seemed the waves to roll*
> *And beat the buckler's verge, and bound the whole.*[12]

And on that classical note he concluded. It was a triumphal end to Webster's distinguished public career. As oratory, critics have declared that it was not one of his greatest efforts; still, as the impassioned plea of a man who desperately loved his country and wanted it to remain whole, it was an unforgettable and deeply moving appeal to reason and patriotic fervor. He made it clear that both the North and the South were responsible for the crisis, and both were responsible for doing what was necessary to save it from dissolution.

Throughout the oration, Webster paused many times so that his words would sink in. Not only did he speak with "very unusual deliberation," said one, but his sentences "were broken into the oddest fragments." He spoke slowly, slower than usual, and his enunciation was "very distinct." The pitch of his voice rose only when he became excited, particularly when speaking about secession. On those occasions, "his eyes appeared like two balls of fire, and his gesticulation indicated the strength of his patriotic impulses." Large drops of perspiration formed on his brow, especially toward the end of his address. And throughout, he stood erect. Most particularly, he stared at Calhoun with "burning eyes."[13]

Although Webster did not discuss Clay's resolutions—he barely mentioned them—he gave the impression that he supported their adoption. Nor did he refer to the president's plan, even though he believed the Senate should start off by admitting California and then go on to the other compromise measures. What he was trying to do was appeal to both the Clay and the Taylor factions in the hope of bringing them together to work out a solution. And his motive had nothing to do with his lifelong ambition to win the presidency. Like Clay, he acted out of a deep love of his country. Senators could tell by the expressions on his face how committed he was to the nation, and they were moved by it. He was an American first and foremost, then a Massachusetts man and a New Englander. "Union is his paramount motive," Philip Hone recorded in his diary, "the Constitution the star by which he steers."[14]

It was a splendid speech that vastly increased Webster's reputation as an orator. Some 200,000 copies were printed, and they were widely distributed. Newspapers in the North and South praised it, and both the *Charleston Mercury* and the *Boston Daily Advertiser* agreed that the speech provided a strong hope that the controversy might be resolved.[15] Webster himself later said that the speech was "probably the most important effort of my life, and as likely as any other to be often referred to."[16]

But it did not take long for criticism to come pouring in. Abolitionists were particularly abusive. There was only one way to account for what Webster had said, insisted Theodore Parker, the renowned abolitionist minister: The speech was "a bid for the Presidency." Others credited it to Webster's lifelong attachment to the wealthy elite, saying he served the "lords of the loom" who profited from the labor of slaves. "Black Dan" did not represent ordinary citizens. He served the rich, North and South. Ralph Waldo Emerson spoke of "Mr. Webster's treachery." But perhaps the most stinging and enduring condemnation came from the Quaker abolitionist John Greenleaf Whittier in his poem "Ichabod."

So fallen! so lost! the light withdrawn
Which once he wore.
The glory from his grey hairs gone, Forevermore![17]

The critics did, however, score one important point. Webster had argued law, history, politics, and geography to make his case. But he had spoken not a word about human rights or moral principles. He had said nothing about the plight of the slaves and their rights as human beings.

In the following weeks, Henry Clay hoped Webster would assist him in his efforts to create a coalition in the Senate that could enact his resolutions, but Black Dan was busy defending himself against the attacks of his critics. He did not have the time to assist the Great Pacificator in building a congressional majority for the compromise. He was otherwise engaged.

Still, Webster's overall plea for moderation and compromise slowly gained ground among Americans, starting with southern Whigs and then circulating among moderates around the nation. Compromise was recognized as the only means by which harmony could be restored and the Union could remain intact. But it had a long way to go before reaching fruition.

—————

On March 31, 1850, John C. Calhoun died, a bitter, frustrated, and disappointed man who loved the Union but loved the South more. He died believing to the depths of his soul in the inevitability of disunion. "Disunion is the only alternative that is left to us," he moaned.[18]

Henry Clay gave a brief eulogy in the Senate. "No man with whom I have ever been acquainted, exceeded him in habits of temperance and regularity, and in all the freedom, frankness, and affability of social intercourse, and in all the tenderness and respect and affection which he manifested" toward his wife, Floride. "No more shall we witness . . . the flashes of that keen and penetrating eye of his," or "that torrent of clear, concise, compact logic . . . which, if it did not always carry conviction to our judgment, commanded our great admiration. . . . I was his senior . . . in years—in nothing else."[19]

And so the Great Triumvirate had spoken, each expressing his own hopes about the future of the Union. With all their efforts they could not solve the basic problem the nation faced. But those efforts, especially Clay's, had helped present secession and civil war. This time, with the nation at the "edge of the precipice," it looked to many that the United States would not endure. And it almost happened.

5

DISASTER

On March 11, 1850, four days after Daniel Webster's Seventh of March speech, William H. Seward of New York rose in the Senate and delivered a scathing rebuttal. Where Webster had brought grandeur and gravity to his oratory, Seward spoke in a monotone, reading from a prepared manuscript, a practice that was frowned upon at that time. And where Webster tried to be accommodating, Seward's opening statement came as something of a shock. It was totally unexpected.

"I am opposed to any such compromise in any and all the forms in which it has been proposed," he announced. "I think all legislative compromises radically wrong and essentially vicious." Why? Because they involved the surrender of "judgment and conscience" and extinguished the rights of the parties to reconsider in the future the decisions made to bring about the compromises. Seward said he was particularly opposed to Clay's resolutions—although he did not mention Clay by name; he just referred to "this one" before the Senate—on the grounds of the "inequality and incongruity of the interests to be compromised." Those in the North would get California, gold, and freedom, he sneered, in return for which they would have to surrender some portion of freedom in the District of Columbia, eastern California, and New Mexico.

The Constitution, in its preamble, Seward declared, dedicated the country to union, justice, defense, welfare, and liberty. But there was "a higher law than the Constitution," in which the "Creator of the universe" bestowed His "domain" on mankind in order to bring the greatest degree of happiness to all. They could not "establish slavery" because it subverted natural rights. It subverted everything the Creator intended for mankind. Slavery, he said, "subverts the principle of democracy, and converts the State into an aristocracy or a despotism." It was contrary to the will of God.

As for Clay's resolutions, Seward would admit California at once and deal with the other issues later. Then he said something that really outraged those who believed in states' rights, many of whom were southerners. The states did not create the Constitution, he declared; the people did. And when they ratified the Constitution, the states surrendered their equality and submitted themselves to the will of the majority "without qualifications or checks." In a Christian nation, slavery was wrong, he insisted. It was immoral. Human law must be brought to the "standard of the law of God . . . and must stand or fall by it."

"I shall vote," he concluded, "for the admission of California directly, without conditions, without qualifications, and without compromise."[1]

And with that announcement, he ended his speech and sat down.

Had Seward been solely intent on raising the wrath of southerners, he surely succeeded. They were appalled by what he said and they condemned him and his arguments, especially his invocation of the Almighty. To bring God into a political debate offended many Americans who felt that religious arguments should never be introduced in any rational discussion of governmental policies. Seward was labeled an "unscrupulous demagogue" who should be consigned to "eternal execration," pontificated one Kentucky editor. A Democratic editor in New Hampshire argued that Seward's doctrines not only guaranteed the destruction of the Union but "of every rational government." His words equating a "higher law" with divine opposition to slavery were condemned as a departure from rational constitutional disputation to something bordering on irresponsible ravings.[2]

Of course, Seward had his defenders, but by and large he had done his reputation and his ambition for the presidency great harm. To bypass the Constitution in a plea for a "higher law" did not sit well with many Americans. Such an argument frightened them because they knew it would surely lead to a bloody confrontation between the opposing sides.

Stephen A. Douglas, chairman of the Senate Committee on Territories, took a moderate stance and now supported Clay's resolutions. He tried to be deferential to both North and South and assured his listeners that the excitement over the possibility of disunion was declining and that "reason" had resumed its supremacy in the council of men. That argument pleased many Americans, especially coming from the chairman of the Senate Committee on Territories, one of the most important and powerful in Congress. It reassured them that a solution could be found through rational discussion, not bloodshed. They would admit California, he said, governments would be created for the new territories, "and thus the controversy will end, and I trust forever."[3]

Douglas's calming voice meant a great deal in Congress and around the country. It was reassuring. His career was also an encouraging factor in the dispute. Born in Vermont, he had moved to New York, then Ohio, and finally settled in Winchester, Illinois, where he taught school and studied law. He ran for public office, served in the U.S. House of Representatives, and in 1847 was finally elected U.S. senator. His career provided the experience and knowledge that made him a formidable legislator. When he spoke, people listened, because they believed he had great command of all the facts involved in the issues. That certitude was largely correct, based on his wide and intense interest in reading. He had a remarkable memory and surprised audiences with his ability to cite facts and figures without having to resort to notes or any other helpful device. Unlike Webster, he did not resort to the kind of oratory that was so fashionable at the time. He was out to win an argument. He sought only one thing: victory.[4]

Throughout the month of March, one senator followed another in presenting their opinions. Southerners complained about the attacks on their way of life, and northerners complained about strengthening the fugitive slave law. Both sides supported or criticized Clay's compromise plan. Some favored the president's proposal; others rejected it as inadequate.

Then Salmon P. Chase of Ohio, a future member of Abraham Lincoln's cabinet and chief justice of the Supreme Court, spoke to the history of attitudes toward slavery. He claimed that the Founders had expected slavery to wither away of its own failings. Unfortunately, that did not happen. "A remarkable change of feeling and action" occurred to prevent the disappearance of slavery. Two reasons, he said, accounted for the change: first, the three-fifths advantage slavery gave southerners in calculating the number of representatives each state could elect to the House; and second, the steady rise of the value of slaves due to the increased production of cotton provided by the invention of the cotton gin. The three-fifths advantage and the cotton gin made slavery profitable both politically and financially.

Like so many other senators, Chase argued in favor of separating California statehood from the other proposals. As for the Texas debt and boundary, he would leave that problem to a later period altogether.[5] But Clay and others kept reminding senators that acting on California alone would destroy any prospect for compromise, and compromise was the only solution to the crisis.

And so week followed week as the debate in the Senate mounted in quarrelsome noise and self-righteous pronouncements without producing a consensus.

In the House more than twenty speeches were delivered during March, with only a third favoring Clay's compromise. Some members warned of the breakup of the Union if southern demands were not met; others tried to convince themselves that the nation was bound together with "hoops of steel" and would never come apart. All of these efforts on both sides added little to clarify the dispute or to find a pathway to a resolution. While mass meetings were being held in New York, Baltimore, and St. Louis in support of the Union, the senators and representatives in Congress continued to pursue a confused and pointless line of bickering and quarreling, leading nowhere.

Finally, on March 25, in an effort to break the impasse, Senator Douglas brought forward two bills: one for the admission of California as a free state, and one for the establishment of territorial governments in Utah (no longer referred to as Deseret because of the Mormon association and the expectation that the bill would fail if that designation was retained) and New Mexico. These bills essentially followed Clay's plan but were not as comprehensive in scope. Then Senator Henry Foote proposed the formation of a select committee of thirteen to prepare a final version of the compromise and lump all the bills together in what Clay had called an omnibus. When faced with a difficult situation, congressmen in both houses were already in the habit of referring such matters to a committee, which would investigate the problem and report back with recommendations at a later date. The thinking behind it was that a committee was more likely to find a solution than the full Senate or House.

Clay had little confidence that such a committee's recommendations would attract a majority of votes, but he was willing to give it a try.

Unfortunately, the administration did nothing to provide guidance or assistance. As early as January 21, President Taylor had made his position clear when he sent a special message to Congress asking the members to do nothing until California applied for admission into the Union. At the same time, he assured Californians that they would decide on a course of action without any interference from Washington. Implicitly, he rejected extending the Missouri Compromise line to the West Coast, since it was expected that California would enter the Union as a free state. As for New Mexico, he asked for patience until a government had been established and the territory had asked for admission. Once New Mexico became a state, the boundary question with Texas could be settled judicially. The Texas debt question would also remain unresolved until some later period.

Do nothing, Taylor advised Congress. Wait. But the situation now demanded answers. An omnibus bill had been proposed. Should there be one bill, combining all the separate issues in Clay's resolutions, or several individual bills? Should California be held separate from the other issues? And was a committee of thirteen the best way to resolve the matter? Here is where the administration could have stepped in and shown leadership. But it remained mute. It did not budge from the position Taylor had announced in his address to Congress. All things considered, Taylor's plan was couched in patriotic terms, but it clearly favored the North and limited southern expansion. California and New Mexico would surely come into the Union as free states. Also Utah, since it was obviously unsuited to slavery. So where did that leave the South? All that section could do was oppose such a settlement.

Apart from the January 21 special message, the administration offered no advice to Congress. There was nothing but silence. "I have never before seen such an Administration," exclaimed Clay. "There is very little co-operation or concord between the two ends of the avenue." Not a single prominent Whig had any "confidential intercourse" with the president. "Seward, it is said, had," Clay wrote, "but, his late Abolition speech has, I presume, cut him off from any such intercourse, as it has eradicated the respect of almost all men for him."[6] Indeed, President Taylor reacted very negatively toward Seward's speech. "Alack," he said, "this is a nice mess Governor Seward has got us into. The speech must be disclaimed at once, authoritatively and decidedly."[7]

So Clay faced a real problem. Should he agree to a single "omnibus" bill, or a series of separate bills? He should have known, given his experience in winning passage of the Missouri Compromise, when it took several separate bills to bring about a resolution. In not recognizing that fact, or acting on it, he probably decided that these were different circumstances and needed a different approach. In any event, during the period between the services held in the Capitol to honor the memory of John C. Calhoun and the three-week interval that occurred when a number of senators accompanied the remains of the deceased to South Carolina, Clay had time to think over his choice. He worried about the fact that the Wilmot Proviso was not included in his resolutions, and therefore might lose northern votes for the compromise. He worried that the southern members would oppose a series of separate measures. He worried over the desire of many to detach California from the other issues and admit it to the Union as a separate, disconnected bill. And, most important, he worried over whether a single bill stood a better chance of preventing a presidential veto than a series of bills in which Taylor could pick and choose which ones he wanted to approve, thus destroying the whole idea of a balance between North and South in terms of what each obtained as a result of the compromise.

So, in April, against his better judgment, but probably on the advice of friends from both parties, Clay chose to support the Foote strategy and go for an omnibus bill. On April 8, he announced his switch on the Senate floor, declaring that he found little "practicality in this idea of total separation of subjects. . . . You may vote against it if you please in toto, because of the bad there is in it, or you may vote for it because you approve of the greater amount of good there is in it."[8]

Clay's announcement surprised many senators, since he and Foote had argued numerous times over how to go about handling the compromise. Thomas Hart Benton took issue with Clay's switch and demanded that California be admitted as a separate measure. He also made it clear that he thought a committee of thirteen was a ludicrous idea. As Benton spoke, his voice grew louder and louder, until he was virtually shaking the walls with the power of his voice. Clay seized upon the opportunity to needle his rival. Cupping his hand around his ear and leaning forward at his desk, Clay called out, "Speak a little louder." The entire chamber burst into laughter.

When Benton finally finished his tirade, Clay rebutted every argument put forth about California's admission and the value of referring the problem to a committee that would produce a single, comprehensive bill. Individual bills, he said, might get vetoed, and he now worried that the attempt to bring California into the Union as a separate item was a ploy by some to satisfy their "own wants" and dismiss all the other parts of the compromise. An omnibus bill concocted by a select committee, he argued, was the best and only way to guarantee passage of the entire package.

Senator Foote jumped into the fray to support Clay and lambasted Benton. Among several criticisms, he denounced the Missouri senator for his criticism of Calhoun's 1849 Southern address. And that was about as much as Benton could take. Seething with rage, he sprang from his seat and headed straight for Foote.

Poor Foote was so terrified that he was about to suffer a physical thrashing that he scrambled toward the vice president's dais, looking for protection. And then it happened: The frightened man pulled out a pistol that was loaded and cocked. The chamber resounded with screams of alarm from witnesses on the floor and in the gallery.

Benton stopped dead in his tracks. Senator Henry Dodge of Wisconsin grabbed him to prevent him from advancing any further. "Let the assassin fire!" screamed Benton. "A pistol has been brought here to assassinate me."

"I brought it here to defend myself," cried Foote, as he surrendered the weapon to Senator Daniel Dickinson of New York.

"Nothing of the kind, sir," Benton snarled. "No assassin has the right to draw a gun on me."

The incident ended abruptly. Tempers cooled, and although there were demands that Foote be expelled from the Senate, nothing came of it. Most senators wished to forget it.[9]

This incident was probably the worst demonstration of the angry, explosive tempers that had pervaded the Senate chamber during these debates. From that point on, things became more rational—and more productive.

⸻

On April 12, Clay turned seventy-three, and the occasion provided a splendid opportunity for the friends of compromise throughout the country to hold rallies and public celebrations demanding that a solution to the crisis be found that would preserve the Union. In Washington, Clay was paid "the compliment of a grand Serenade." At ten in the evening, some of Clay's friends, accompanied by the Marine Corps band, assembled under his hotel window and saluted him with a medley of patriotic songs. When he finally appeared, he answered their cries for a speech by again reciting his great love for his country and assuring the crowd that somehow he would work out a resolution to the present dispute. At that moment, he was the undisputed hero of the country, a statesman who seemed to embody the assurances the people wished to hear.[10]

One way Clay hoped to achieve his goal was in the regular caucus meetings that he chaired. What he tried to do, and finally succeeded in doing, was to put together a supporting coalition of southern Whigs and leaders of the border states, together with conservative and liberal northern Democrats. Conservative Democrats in the group looked to Lewis Cass for leadership, while more liberal northern Democrats followed Stephen A. Douglas. Under Clay's guidance, these several factions united on April 18 and approved the formation of Foote's Committee of Thirteen to consider all the questions dealing with slavery and the territories.

The following day, the Senate selected the members of this committee: six Democrats and six Whigs. Henry Clay was chosen as the thirteenth member; he was also named chairman. He received twenty-eight votes, against Benton, John Bell of Tennessee, and Willie P. Mangum of North Carolina, who obtained one vote each (there were also four blank ballots cast). The vote was a ringing tribute to the Great Compromiser and the respect and admiration the senators had for him. In addition to Clay, the committee consisted of three northern Whigs (Webster, Samuel S. Phelps of Vermont, and James Cooper of Pennsylvania); three southern Whigs (Mangum, Bell, and John M. Berrien of Georgia); three northern Democrats (Cass, Daniel S. Dickinson of New York, and Jesse D. Bright of Indiana); and three southern Democrats (Mason, William R. King of Alabama, and Solomon W. Downs of Louisiana).

Stephen A. Douglas refused to join the Committee of Thirteen because he strongly opposed the use of an omnibus. He was certain it would fail.[11] Previously, before the Committee of Thirteen had been proposed, he had written several bills on March 25 involving the admission of California, the creation of territorial governments for New Mexico and Utah, and the settlement of the Texas boundary. He showed them to Clay and Cass and asked whether they should be separate bills or combined into one. Clay and Cass both advised him to keep them separate—which is what he did. But two weeks later, in agreeing to the omnibus bill, Clay had effectively changed his mind. Douglas disagreed with Clay's decision and opposed the omnibus as "unwise & unnecessary." He demonstrated rare insight.[12]

Naturally, Clay dominated the committee once it began its meetings, but he frequently yielded on minor procedural matters in an effort to promote harmony within the group. Still, he was outvoted on one important point. The majority agreed that slavery must not be disallowed by territorial legislatures, thus affirming the southern position that the Constitution protected slave property until a territory became a state. This action undercut Clay's recognition of the binding force of Mexican law that forbade slavery in the territories annexed by the United States. For a solid week the committee argued and debated before finally agreeing to this majority recommendation. The members then dispersed and left it to Clay to write the final report. On April 25, he went into seclusion at the home of his friend Charles Benedict Calvert near Bladensburg, Maryland, where he prepared the final document while hoping to recover from a severe cold that had troubled him for weeks.[13]

After writing the report, Clay prepared to deliver it to the Senate. On Wednesday, May 8, he presented the report to a chamber packed with members and visitors. The measure linked the admission of California as a free state with the establishment of territorial governments for New Mexico and Utah. At the same time it denied these territories the right to legislate on slavery. It also fixed the boundary of Texas, with compensation to that state for relinquishing all claim to any portion of New Mexico. As a separate item the report called for a fugitive slave law that included two important amendments: the first required slaveholders to produce documentary evidence for their claim of loss; and the second provided for trial by jury if the alleged fugitive so requested—but it was to be held in the state from which he or she had fled. While this item was expected to win southern votes, the amendments sought to legally protect the runaways from illegal procedures. Finally, the report recommended the abolition of the slave trade in the District of Columbia.[14]

Although several members of the committee disagreed over certain proposals—and they did not hesitate to present their differences to the other senators—Clay himself complimented all the participants for their outstanding performance. "I have never been associated," he said, "with gentlemen on any great and momentous occasion in which a spirit of more kindness, more conciliation, and more of a disposition to listen and to give effect . . . than was presented during the whole of our session."[15]

Unfortunately, the bill, as described in the report, did not give senators much choice. Either they swallow the bill whole, every part of it, or reject it completely. It turned out to be a prescription for defeat.

The following Monday, Clay rose in the Senate and went over the report at length. The committee, he said, had joined the two bills presented by Senator Douglas on March 25, namely, the admission of California and the establishment of territorial governments for New Mexico and Utah. Then he assured the senators that the decision to restrict the territories from legislating on slavery was unimportant. What he hid from them was his intention of restoring popular sovereignty to the bill during the course of the debate. He was trying to keep everybody happy at the outset of the discussion and in time make necessary changes so as to allow territorial legislatures the right to introduce or forbid slavery within their jurisdictions, ensuring passage of the entire package. However, he did ask the North to give up any mention of the Wilmot Proviso, because the South felt that once Congress initiated legislation on slavery, there was "no seeing where it is to end." Clay offered the North "compensations" in the form of a resolution involving "two truths, one of law and one of fact," namely, that slavery "does not exist by law," and that it was "not likely to be introduced" into the territories because of the unsuitable terrain.

Then Clay took on the role of play-actor, inventing emotions and attitudes to serve his purpose of winning senatorial approval. In an emotional outburst, he cried out that no measure dealing with the territories could ever be enacted without producing "scenes of the most painful and unpleasant character." After that explosion, his face suddenly brightened and his voice mellowed. He was happy to say that he had witnessed a "gratifying change" on both sides. The "North, the glorious North, has come to the rescue of this Union of ours. She has displayed a disposition to abate in her demands." That was news to some northerners in the chamber, but they delighted in his performance.

Clay continued. The "South—the glorious South—no less glorious than her neighbor section of the Union—has also come to the rescue. The minds of men have moderated; passion has given place to reason everywhere." Rather than allow the territories to "shift for themselves," as proposed by President Taylor, the committee had agreed to provide them with "adequate and appropriate governments."

Following that snide remark about the president, Clay followed up with a similar swipe at Senator Seward. The fugitive slave bill, he acknowledged, would not please those in the free states who asserted "that there is a higher law—a divine law—a natural law—which entitles a man, under whose roof a runaway has come, to give him assistance, and succor, and hospitality." What is the difference, he asked, between protecting a fugitive and invading a plantation and stealing him outright? It was exactly the same thing. Without mentioning Seward by name, Clay denounced the "wild, reckless and abominable theories, which strike at the foundation of all property and threaten to crush in ruins the fabric of civilized society."[16]

The performance was one of Clay's most theatrical—and most effective. He obviously appealed to both sections for their assistance in obtaining a compromise, and he congratulated them for doing what was best for the Union. Still, it was not enough to prevent Ultras, namely, the extremists, in the North and South from denouncing the proposed bill. By and large, southern Whigs and northern Democrats followed their economic or political interests and supported the measure, but southern Democrats and northern Whigs, for the same reasons, opposed it. Leading the opposition was Jefferson Davis of Mississippi, a southern Democrat, and William H. Seward, a northern Whig. But one northern Democrat stood aloof. Senator Stephen A. Douglas did not believe the bill could pass as a single package. In its present form, he insisted, a majority in favor could not be mustered. The bill would have to be disassembled to allow each senator the prerogative of voting in favor of one issue but against another.

Two days later, on May 15, the formal debate on the omnibus bill began in the Senate, and immediately the strategy of the opposition became obvious: Introduce amendments and amendments on amendments; introduce calls for adjournment, recess, postponements; demand explanations of meaning or interpretation of particular clauses; and introduce extraneous matters that had nothing to do with the compromise. All these maneuvers kept Clay responding daily, fighting off these "disunionists," as he called them.

He was especially concerned about two matters that he knew made the bill vulnerable: California, which once admitted in a separate bill would encourage senators to scrap the rest of the compromise; and drawing an acceptable boundary for Texas. For some senators California was their only real interest; once its statehood request passed without any linkage to the other issues, they would be satisfied and would disregard everything else, thus killing the compromise. And the Texas boundary question involved her debt and New Mexico and could easily become a battleground between North and South.

Senator Benton was particularly eager to separate California and admit it as a free state into the Union. As a result, he tangled frequently with Clay over the issue, and their language became heated and more disagreeable over the next two months. At one point, for example, Clay's anger boiled over and he accused Benton of calumny. He "hurled" his charge with "scorn and indignation" that Benton could "stick it in his casket of calumnies, where he has many other things of the same sort."[17]

Throughout the month of June, twenty-eight senators attempted to amend the omnibus package, only a few of which succeeded. Perhaps the most important of their amendments was one offered by Senator Berrien authorizing the territorial legislatures to protect slave property in case a judicial decision jeopardized it.[18] This was important to southerners in preventing the possibility of judicial interference, especially in the North.

———

Over in the House, the debate produced long-winded harangues both for and against the compromise. Fifty-eight members carried on from May 8 to June 11, some supporting Clay's proposals, others favoring the president's plan, and a few advocating inclusion of the Wilmot Proviso. Most of the time these men spoke to a near-empty chamber. At one point it was suggested that there should have been a joint committee of the House and Senate to prepare a compromise bill, but nothing came of that suggestion. By the end of June it looked as though Congress was going nowhere—as usual.[19]

While the House wrestled over what action to take, the Senate continued its debate, with Jefferson Davis arguing for the extension of the Missouri Compromise line to the Pacific Ocean. Clay disagreed. The 36°30' line was an old solution to a different quarrel over slavery, he said. That solution would not do in 1850. If Congress had the right to introduce slavery in territories where it did not exist, such as California and New Mexico, did it not follow that Congress could also prohibit slavery in any territory? Was that what Davis wished to achieve? Hardly. And to Davis's complaint that the compromise provided nothing for the South, Clay answered by reminding the Mississippi senator of the "total absence" of any mention of congressional action on slavery, such as the Wilmot Proviso, in the compromise. For years the South had complained about the proviso and how it must be rejected from all legislation having to do with slavery. Well, exclaimed Clay, that demand had been achieved. "The proviso is not in the bill," because the committee distinctly declared that the proviso was "totally destitute . . . of any practical import." Congress must not and would not act on slavery in the territories. It must be left to the people living in the territories to decide whether or not they wished to have the institution introduced. "The bill," he insisted, "is neither southern nor northern. It is equal; it is fair; it is a compromise."[20]

The nation demanded compromise, Clay said once again. He spoke slowly and with special emphasis on each word. It could not survive another year of "this agitation, this distraction, this exasperation" between the North and the South. "Instead of healing and closing the wounds of the country, instead of stopping the effusion of blood, it will flow in even still greater quantities."[21] If they failed to provide a solution to the agitation, they would surely create the makings of a bloodbath.

———

In the many speeches Clay delivered over the following weeks, he sometimes stumbled when his emotions ran high. One of his tactical blunders came in a speech on May 21 in which he fool-ishly attacked the president, thereby announcing to the country that the Whig Party was badly split. He contrasted the presi-dent's plan with that of the committee and said that he would describe what Taylor had proposed with a "smile." He was that contemptuous. The nation suffered from five wounds[22]—a figure of speech he used repeatedly—and then Clay raised his hand and ticked them off, "one, two, three, four, five." What would the president do? Heal only one, while the others con-tinued to fester, "even if it should produce death itself."

Clay knew his speech did his party great harm, but the pres-ident by his plan "left me no other alternative," he insisted. He was fighting for the life of his country. Taylor's plan, he be-lieved, would destroy the nation. And with each succeeding speech he lacerated Taylor further—and he suffered the con-sequences. "War, open war, undisguised war, was made by the administration," he growled.[23] Said Daniel Webster: "I think Mr. Clay is in danger of eclipsing his glory. Why attack the President?"[24]

The administration was not Clay's only foe. The Great Com-promiser told his family that he was besieged by a coalition of opponents. "The Administration, the Abolitionists, the Ultra

Southern men, and the timid Whigs of the North are all combined against it [the Omnibus Bill]. Against such a combination, it will be wonderful if it should succeed."[25] Wonderful,
indeed. But hardly likely.

———

While Congress busily debated over a possible compromise,
the delegates to the Nashville Convention began arriving in the
city, anxious to let the nation know exactly what they thought
about the current crisis. They had expected to hold their meetings in the Odd Fellows Hall, but so many delegates appeared
that they had to move to larger quarters. The trustees of the
McKendree Methodist Church offered them the use of their
building, a structure that could hold 1,500 people. The con-
ventioneers quickly and gratefully accepted the offer, and on
Monday, June 3, 1850, former governor Aaron V. Brown of
Tennessee called the meeting to order.

It was well attended. Nine southern states were represented—
Alabama, Arkansas, Florida, Georgia, Mississippi, South Carolina, Tennessee, Texas, and Virginia—with Alabama sending
the largest contingent of delegates, 22 in all. South Carolina sent
17, Mississippi 11. The relatively new state of Florida dispatched 4 men to the convention, and although Texas had
elected 8, only 1 showed up in Nashville on time. Louisiana refused to pay for its delegation and so went unrepresented. The
Tennessee legislature had failed to provide election procedures,
so 101 men, mostly chosen at county meetings, took part in the
proceedings.[26]

A large number of visitors also attended the sessions and virtually participated in the discussions by the applause and vocal reactions they provided in response to remarks by various speakers. They were so vitally interested in what the convention would do that they could not restrain themselves from expressing approval or disapproval of what was said on the convention floor.

After taking care of organizational matters, the delegates addressed two lengthy sets of resolutions. At the outset, several delegates wanted it made clear that they had come to "preserve unimpaired the Union" through the "preservation inviolate of the Constitution . . . which made the Union."[27] That was an encouraging sign, but the rights of the South were articulated again and again. The members repeated the general sentiment in the South that the people of that region and their institutions and lifestyle were being discriminated against. After many speeches and demands that the southern states have equal access to the territories, the delegates passed a set of resolutions and an address that stopped short of advocating secession. The resolutions criticized Clay's plan and opted for extending the 36°30' line to the Pacific Ocean but offered nothing new by way of resolving the many other issues involved in the controversy. The address was much more harsh in its language than the resolutions, but it did not call for disunion. Instead the members chose to wait and see what Congress would do, after which it would reconvene in Nashville in November to take action after Congress had recessed.

The failure of the Ultras at the Convention to win support for immediate secession helped encourage moderates in Congress to renew their efforts to adopt a compromise. But the problem for them, especially for the administration, became more complicated. Confident of Taylor's backing, the leaders in New Mexico opted for immediate statehood under a free-state constitution. However, this was not part of the president's plan as recommended in his special message to Congress in January. Furthermore, these New Mexico leaders proposed boundaries that were totally unacceptable to Texas; and in response Texas threatened to dispatch troops to Santa Fe to establish its territorial rights. Violence now seemed likely.

Even more worrisome was the deteriorating relationship between Clay and the administration. The "breach between the Administration and me," wrote the senator to his wife on July 6, "is getting wider and wider. Their conduct is generally condemned. They seem utterly regardless of public feeling and opinion, and blindly rushing on to their own ruin, if not the ruin of their Country."[28]

Then, things changed suddenly and dramatically. On July 4, the president attended an Independence Day celebration at the unfinished Washington Monument and listened in blistering heat to an hour-long harangue by Senator Foote. When it ended, the president was debilitated and soaked with perspiration. Verging on dehydration and overcome by an intense thirst, Taylor hurried back to the White House, where he consumed a great deal of raw vegetables and fruit—the kind "made for four footed animals & not Bipeds"[29]—and washed it all down with ice water. The following day he showed the first signs of cholera morbus, which proceeded to get worse each day until he died in agony on July 9, 1850. He was succeeded by the vice president, Millard Fillmore. And with that sudden, tragic sequence of events, one of the worst enemies of Clay's compromise plan was eliminated.

Indeed, the Kentucky senator contended that Taylor's death would "favor the passage of the Compromise bill." The accession of Fillmore of New York was particularly auspicious in that he and Clay had had a long friendship. The new president showed the Great Compromiser all the attention and access denied him by the Taylor administration. "My relations with the new Chief are intimate and confidential," boasted Clay.[30] They met often and privately. Also, William H. Seward's influence with the administration ended abruptly with Taylor's death. He and Fillmore, both New Yorkers, bitterly disliked each other.

Clay was elated by Fillmore's elevation. Now there was no more talk of vetoes or weakening the compromise with amendments. However, the Kentucky senator did wish to make one change. It had been the decision of the Committee of Thirteen to restrict the territorial legislatures from enacting any measure regarding slavery. Senator Douglas had already tried and failed to include popular sovereignty. Now Clay asked him to try again. Circumstances had changed considerably in the past few weeks and he now thought a motion to strike out the amendment forbidding action by the territorial legislatures regarding slavery stood a good chance of passage.

But Douglas preferred to operate behind the scenes and designated Moses Norris, the Democratic senator from New Hampshire, to introduce the amendment. And on July 31, it passed the Senate by a vote of 32 to 20. Several factors accounted for this clear and important victory. First, it was known and reported that Fillmore favored a compromise with popular sovereignty; second, there was an increased demand by the public for passage of a compromise; third, a reduction of tensions had resulted from the adjournment of the Nashville Convention without a call for secession; and fourth, New Mexico had fashioned a constitution without slavery. So the amendment was adopted, and territorial legislatures were now permitted to forbid or permit slavery subject only to a possible veto by the governor or an objection by Congress.[31]

It now appeared that the omnibus would indeed win passage in the Senate. And Clay gave it one last and mighty heave on July 22. It was his best effort during the entire debate. "I never heard Clay more eloquent," the Jacksonian editor Francis Blair later told Van Buren. He never exhibited "greater resources of mind."[32] In several heartfelt, emotional outbursts, Clay appealed to the patriotic, nationalistic, moralistic feelings of his audience and frequently won their cheers, laughter, and applause. At times the responses from Clay's listeners became so raucous that the president of the Senate threatened to clear the galleries. The Great Compromiser gave a long speech, one of the longest he ever delivered, and it totally convinced many of those who heard him that a compromise must be enacted.

He spoke of the late president with respect, calling him "an honest man . . . a brave man" whose actions in many areas had met with his "hearty and cordial concurrence." But as to his plan for the solution of the present crisis, Clay totally, yet "with the most perfect respect for his memory," disagreed. The late president wished to bring New Mexico into the Union as a state, but New Mexico was not ready for statehood. Even the New

Mexicans knew that. What they wanted, and what they needed, was a territorial government.

As for the "omnibus, as it is called," said Clay, in one of his more eloquent outbursts, "I thank, from the bottom of my heart, the enemy of the bill who gave it that denomination. The omnibus is the vehicle of the people, of the masses of the people. . . . We have no Africans or Abolitionists in our omnibus— no disunionists or Free Soilers, no Jew or Gentile. Our passengers consist of Democrats and Whigs, who, seeing the crisis of their common country . . . have met together . . . to compare their opinions upon this great measure of reconciliation and harmony."

In the course of his speech, Clay frequently took note of criticisms from various senators, particularly the abolitionist John P. Hale of New Hampshire and Jefferson Davis of Mississippi. Abolitionists, said Clay, "live by agitation. It is their meat, their bread, the air which they breathe." And if they saw a measure that would increase their meat, bread, and air, "do you not believe that they would hail it as a blessing?" This use of Hale's name as a pun to make a point caused the chamber to burst into laughter.

Clay particularly deplored Davis's "expression which filled all of us with profound regret" when he "spoke of New Mexico being adapted to the *breeding* of slaves." Such talk "about the cotton power, the lords of the loom, and the breeding of slaves" was suitable for "the bar-rooms of cross-roads taverns, but I never hoped or expected to hear upon the floor of the Senate such epithets applied to the great manufacturers of the North and the cotton-growers of the South." The country was not built upon, nor would it be "harmonized" by, the use of such slogans as "the slave power" and the "money power." Using any such epithets diminished the reputation of the nation as the home of free and God-fearing people.

Clay then went on to explain once again what each section of the country would gain or lose if the omnibus bill passed. The North, he said, would gain the admission of California as a free state and the "high probability" of New Mexico and Utah "remaining or becoming" free territory. It would avoid any introduction of slavery into these territories "by the authority of Congress." It would secure the abolition of the slave trade in the District of Columbia. As for the South, he said, passage of the omnibus would avoid the assertion by Congress of the "dangerous principle" contained in the Wilmot Proviso. It would obtain nine hundred miles of territory within Texas and implement an "efficient" fugitive slave law. Finally, the bill would silence agitation about slavery in the District of Columbia. The South would get no territory in California, New Mexico, or Utah that would be useful for the introduction of slavery, Clay acknowledged, but for this "She cannot blame Congress, but must upbraid Nature's law and Nature's God!"

Turning to the southern senators, he asked this question: If slavery would never exist in those territories, "Why contend for it?" Two hundred years from now, if not sooner, posterity would look back with astonishment that they threatened the existence of the Union over something that would never and could never exist. From "the bottom of my soul," Clay cried, the omnibus bill "is the reunion of this Union. I believe it is the dove of peace, taking its aerial flight from the dome of the Capitol, carries the glad tidings of assured peace and restored harmony to all the remotest extremities of this distracted land." He begged the senators to rid themselves of personal resentments, petty jealousies, and individual desires and "think alone of our God, our country, our consciences, and our glorious Union."

Clay concluded this magnificent address by stating that if Kentucky "unfurls the banner of resistance unjustly," he himself would never fight under that banner. "I owe a permanent allegiance to the whole Union—a subordinate one to my own State." If Kentucky were to engage in any action against the Union, "never, never will I engage with her in such a cause." Should South Carolina or any other state "hoist the flag of disunion and rebellion," patriots and gallant men from all the other states would respond. "Thousands, tens of thousands of Kentuckians would flock to the standard of their country to dissipate and repress the rebellion."

Clay swelled to his conclusion. "These are my sentiments," he declared, and having said that, he dropped his arms to his sides and cried, "Make the most of them."[33]

The entire Senate burst into loud and prolonged applause when Clay ended his oration. His listeners were deeply moved. Here before them was a statesman who loved his country and was prepared to sacrifice his life in protecting it from harm. The *National Intelligencer* of July 23 declared that Clay had "surpassed even his ancient fame as a powerful, impassioned and impressive debater."[34] His eloquence brought tears to the eyes of both men and women. The walls of the chamber shook with jeers, applause, and the stamping of feet.

Clay collapsed into his seat, perspiration pouring down his face. What "a magnificent effort," wrote Grace Greenwood in one of her regular letters to the Philadelphia *Saturday Evening Post*. "At his advanced age, to be able to stand up and speak so eloquently and so powerfully for three hours of an oppressively hot day, proves the Kentucky statesman to be one of the wonders of our time and country."[35]

Indeed. To many present in the room, it seemed as though the omnibus bill would be enacted without further delay.

———

And then it happened. Suddenly, on July 31, the omnibus "went to pieces all at once." What triggered the disaster was the Texas boundary question. It started when Senator James W. Bradbury of Maine proposed that the boundary question be entrusted to a joint U.S.-Texas commission—which made a lot of sense. Georgia Senator William C. Dawson added a modification stipulating that New Mexico would not have jurisdiction of the territory east of the Rio Grande until the commission had agreed on the boundary line. But in his concern that New Mexico might object strenuously to this restriction—the imbalance it might cause, in that New Mexico was restricted but not Texas—Senator James A. Pearce of Maryland, a fervent supporter of compromise, declared that Dawson's modification was "cranky, lop-eared, crippled, deformed." He therefore moved that it be stricken out. He felt he could propose something less controversial.

In an instant, Clay recognized the danger of Pearce's motion in that it would alienate southerners. He jumped to his feet, begged Pearce to withdraw his motion, and said there were other ways to deal with possible imbalances. But Pearce would not back off. He stood his ground and demanded a vote. To Clay's horror, the vote to strike out the modification carried by the count of 33 to 22. Nineteen northerners and fourteen southerners voted for the Pearce amendment; only six Whigs, including Clay, voted against it.

The linkage between the various components of the compromise was now gone. And with that disaster, the rest of the omnibus soon collapsed. Senator David L. Yulee of Florida moved to strike out everything having to do with Texas, and his motion passed by one vote, 29 to 28. Sixteen northern and fourteen southern votes accounted for the passage of Yulee's amendment. Once Texas was shot down, California followed on a motion by Senator David R. Atchison of Missouri, 34 to 25. Southerners had ganged up against California once the Texas boundary issue was eliminated, and that vote left the omnibus in ruins. Ten northern and twenty-four southern senators voted for the Atchison motion.[36] It was now clear that the various territorial issues had stood a far better chance of passage had they been dealt with separately rather than as an omnibus motion.

The shattered Clay slumped in his seat, looking "as melancholy as Caius Marius over the ruins of Carthage."[37] Then he slowly rose from his seat and walked out of the chamber.

"The omnibus is overturned," rejoiced Thomas Hart Benton, "and all the passengers spilled out but one. We have but Utah left—all gone but Utah." Several other senators laughed over what had happened. The "Mormons alone got thru' living," said one, "the Christians all jumped out." Abolitionists and Ultras congratulated themselves, and Seward danced around the room. Benton could hardly restrain himself. "*He* had routed *Clay*! He had smashed the omnibus to atoms."[38]

Clay was devastated. But he should have known from his experience with the Missouri Compromise that an omnibus bill had little chance of success. Senators could not be given a choice of the omnibus or nothing. They needed the privilege of voting for some measures in the package and against others. But Clay was sure that only a single package would dispel southern fears, and that was his mistake. Douglas, who personally regretted the collapse of the omnibus despite the fact that he had little hope for its success, explained what had happened: "By combining the measures into one Bill the Committee united the opponents of each measure instead of securing the friends of each."[39]

The next day, Clay returned to the Senate and blasted Pearce for deliberately destroying the compromise. He was especially "indignant at his Southern allies" who had voted for the several measures that crushed the omnibus. Nevertheless, he was prepared to pursue another course of action to win approval for his proposal. "I am willing now to see them pass separate and distinct, and I hope they may be passed so without that odious proviso which has created such a sensation in every quarter of the Union." And then he left the chamber and left Washington. He went off on a vacation to recover from a series of respiratory infections that would eventually kill him. He "has gone north," reported the *National Intelligencer*, "in order to recruit, by a few days rest, his exhausted strength."[40]

"And so the Omnibus is smashed—wheels, axils and body—nothing left but a single plank termed Utah," wrote Horace Greeley in the *New York Tribune* on August 2, 1850. "I even saw the gallant driver abandoning the wreck between six and seven this evening, after having done all that man could do to retrieve, or rather to avert the disaster." It now seemed hopeless. "There is nothing left but to grin and bear it."

6

DOUGLAS TO THE
RESCUE

A broken man headed north. When Clay reached Philadelphia, a crowd gathered to greet him. A real omnibus tried to get through the cheering masses but could not and came to a full stop. Clay laughed. "That omnibus is like the omnibus I left at Washington," he said; "it didn't get through." His sense of humor had obviously remained intact. As the crowd quieted, he explained that he had adopted the omnibus approach because he thought it had a better chance of passage. Now he knew better and hoped for the enactment of each part of his compromise as a separate bill.

But, to a very large extent, the failure was his. His quarrels with those who questioned his proposals, and especially his denunciation of Pearce, who favored his compromise and was trying to work out a better solution to the New Mexico boundary question, did not help. Later, he acknowledged the efforts of Daniel Webster, Lewis Cass, Henry S. Foote, Daniel S. Dickinson, James Cooper, Jesse D. Bright, Solomon W. Downs, Willie P. Mangum, and other members of the Committee of Thirteen in helping him in his efforts to get his compromise through the Senate.

Now, as he headed toward Newport, Rhode Island, to splash in the seawater and soak up the August sun in the hope of finding a cure for his persistent cough, he heard from the crowds who attended his passage through their communities how much they appreciated his efforts on their behalf and how much they, too, desperately wanted Congress to find a solution that would save the Union.[1] Now they faced possible secession and civil war, and it frightened them more than anything that had occurred in the recent past.

———

Without Clay's direction, the Senate found a new leader: Stephen A. Douglas, chairman of the Committee on Territories. He had always believed that the omnibus was nothing but a vehicle to unite all the opponents of compromise into an unbeatable phalanx; only through the separate consideration of each part of Clay's compromise, he said, could success be found. To begin the process he was sure California would get through the Senate as a free state with little difficulty, and he promised to bring it forward as a separate bill as soon as possible. Over seven working days he prepared a series of individual measures. First, after he arranged a slight adjustment of Utah's southern boundary, he won its passage in the Senate on August 1. Then he introduced a bill for the admission of California. Meanwhile, he and Pearce fashioned a new Texas boundary bill that conceded 33,333 more square miles of territory to the state than had been authorized by the omnibus, while still leaving New Mexico with all its occupied territory. Upon agreeing to this arrangement, Texas would receive 10 million dollars. This modified measure passed the Senate on August 9, and it now seemed very likely that the remainder of the compromise package would follow in short order.

"Hail Liberty and Union and Domestic Peace!" cried the *National Intelligencer* on August 10. "Hail the return of Government from its long aberration back to its just sphere of action and usefulness."

Then, on August 13, the Senate agreed to the admission of California as a free state by a vote of 34 to 18, a whopping majority of 16 votes. After the California and Texas questions, said Douglas, "we shall then take up the Bill for New Mexico & pass it just as I reported it four months ago." When they had passed all the bills, he declared, they would "collectively be Mr. Clay's Compromise."[2]

The day following the California vote, the New Mexico bill passed overwhelmingly, 27 to 10. And on August 23, the fugitive slave bill went to its third reading by a vote of 27 to 12. It passed three days later on a simple voice vote.[3]

It is remarkable how quickly these bills won passage in the Senate. Obviously the members were weary and wanted to be done with the debate. In just a few weeks Douglas had resurrected all the essential parts of the omnibus and obtained Senate approval for their enactment. It was quite an achievement—and the credit all belonged to Douglas. He assembled winning combinations of Democrats, Whigs, and Free Soilers—northerners and southerners. For the California vote, 17 Democrats, 15 Whigs, and 2 Free Soilers favored the bill, while 14 Democrats and 4 Whigs opposed it. Those voting for California's admission included 28 northerners and 6 southerners, while those voting against the bill included 14 northerners and 4 southerners. With respect to the New Mexico vote, 19 Democrats and 8 Whigs approved it, and these included 11 northerners and 16 southerners, while 3 Democrats, 6 Whigs, and 1 Free Soiler opposed the bill, all from the North.

The California bill, the territorial governments, and the Texas debt bills constituted the core of the compromise. Their passage was essential for any final solution to the crisis. The fugitive slave law was a sine qua non for southerners and attracted 15 southern Democrats, 9 southern Whigs, and 3 northern Democrats, while 3 northern Democrats, 8 northern Whigs, and 1 Free Soiler voted against it—a clearly delineated sectional vote, which did not cause as much trouble as feared but later generated considerable public opposition in the North. In each of these votes there were abstentions, particularly among abolitionists, such as Hale, and Ultras, including Davis. They refused to have their names associated with particular bills that they detested.[4] Where the omnibus had united opponents of compromise, the presentation of separate bills united various groupings of senators, North and South, to win their passage.

By the time Henry Clay returned from his three-week vacation in Rhode Island, all these measures had been passed under the leadership of Senator Douglas. What remained to be enacted was the District of Columbia slave trade bill, which outlawed the sale of slaves in Washington. Finally, on September 16, it, too, won approval under Clay's "personal guidance."[5] The vote was 33 to 19, and those nineteen were all southerners.

There were six bills in all, and of these only four senators supported all six measures. The gallant four included Sam Houston, Democrat of Texas; August C. Dodge, Democrat of Iowa; Daniel Sturgeon, Democrat of Pennsylvania; and John Wales, Whig of Delaware. An additional seven senators approved five of the six bills and abstained from voting on a sixth bill. These seven consisted of Steven A. Douglas, Democrat of Illinois; Lewis Cass, Democrat of Michigan; Jesse D. Bright, Democrat of Indiana; Alpheus Felch, Democrat of Michigan; Moses Norris, Democrat of New Hampshire; James Shields, Democrat of Illinois; and Presley Spruance, Whig of Delaware.[6] Douglas was out of town on business when the fugitive slave bill was passed.[7]

Quite obviously, it was the Democrats in the Senate who provided the votes to win the final compromise. The Whigs were split not only between the North and the South but within each of the two sections of the country. Their decline and eventual disappearance as a viable political party was now a certainty.

These several bills won approval in the Senate because they cut across political and sectional lines. Enough men in the chamber recognized the importance of compromise in ending the crisis and set aside their individual prejudices for the sake of preventing possible bloodshed.

Among Democrats, several senators took credit for the passage of the Compromise of 1850. Douglas never boasted that he had put together all the issues necessary by which each side of the dispute would give up something in order to gain something. However, he did claim authorship of the bills involving the Texas debt and the territorial governments. What Clay did was to find all the necessary parts of a workable compromise and to link them together wherein the passage of each part was dependent upon the enactment of all. But Clay failed to win passage of the compromise because he opted for an omnibus solution, a method that Douglas recognized as fatally flawed. It was Douglas who won passage of the compromise, and he rightly took credit for that achievement. But he also readily acknowledged what Clay had accomplished. Years later in a speech in Cincinnati, he explained what the Kentuckian had done that made a difference. "All the Union men, North and South, Whigs and Democrats, for the period of six months were assembled in Caucus every day, with Clay in the chair, Cass upon his right hand, Webster upon his left hand, and the Whigs and Democrats arranged on either side," he said.[8] And under Clay's guiding hand, they worked ceaselessly and "harmoniously," finally forging and winning approval for the compromise and thereby preventing secession. Foote, Cass, and Dickinson have also received credit for their contributions in obtaining passage of the six bills.[9]

That final compromise, as passed in the Senate, constituted, in Douglas's words, "one grand scheme of conciliation and adjustment" in which all the measures, not just one or a few, but all, needed to be passed. As a consequence, he said, "neither section has triumphed over the other"; each retained "its honor and its rights."[10]

———

But the crisis did not disappear just because the bills had passed the Senate. The struggle then switched to the House of Representatives, where for weeks, in the blistering heat of a particularly hot and humid summer, the members screamed and ranted at one another. Now that the upper house had passed the compromise, a number of senators regularly appeared on the floor of the House to lend whatever assistance they could to getting the measures approved. Douglas, Foote, Cass, and Clay, among others, offered help and advice. Douglas singled out Linn Boyd of Kentucky, chairman of the House Committee on Territories, and provided him with encouragement and much-needed information.

Not until August 28 and 29 did the House make a real effort to bring the quarreling to a halt. On the 28th, Boyd offered what was called a "little omnibus" when he proposed an amendment combining a bill dealing with the settlement of the Texas boundary and its debt with another bill for the New Mexico boundary. On the 29th, southern Ultras tried to kill it by referring it to the Committee of the Whole, but Speaker Cobb ruled against them. In defending his "little omnibus," Boyd accused his colleagues of not doing their duty as the people demanded. Instead they did nothing. "I am astonished," he cried, "at the patience with which our constituents have borne our procrastination"—a charge that could be repeated many times in the future, right to this very day. "Every man in this House" ought to resign, Boyd blasted, and let the people "send here Representatives better disposed to do their duty and to save the Union."[11]

So, for the next several days, the struggle continued amid "great confusion" in the chamber and "constant disorder." There were repeated demands for a roll call—eleven, to be exact—but the Speaker managed to ward them off and keep control. President Fillmore met privately with Whig members and used what influence he had with them to win their support for the compromise. Clay, too, pressed his friends to help. "It was an exciting time," reported the *New York Herald* on September 7, "and much confusion prevailed." Members left their desks and circulated around the chamber, talking up the compromise or denouncing it according to their commitment.

Finally, on September 6, the engrossment[12] of the "little omnibus" came up for a final vote. As the roll call proceeded, members crowded around the clerk's desk to see which way the vote was going. The count ended and Cobb rapped his gavel to announce the result.

"Ayes 107," he cried. Then, he halted when he saw a latecomer enter the chamber and record his vote.

"Yeas 108," Cobb corrected himself, "nays 98."[13]

The House exploded with cheers, shouts, whistles, and foot stamping. For all intents and purposes the Union was saved: The Compromise of 1850 had passed.

It came as an anticlimax when the "little omnibus" itself passed, 108 to 97.

The following day, Saturday, September 7, the adoption of the California (150–56) and Utah (97–85) bills came with little debate or significant opposition.

When *all* the affirmative votes in the House for each of the five bills were added together, it showed that the compromise had passed with 305 Democratic votes and 262 Whig votes. Of the negative votes, 176 were Democrats and 168 Whigs.[14]

On Saturday evening people celebrated by firing one hundred guns at Washington Monument Square and discharging rockets from the Mall. A crowd, accompanied by the Marine Corps band, marched to Clay's hotel to thank him for putting the compromise together. But, once again, he had gone to Calvert's country home to rest and regain his strength. So the marchers turned around and demonstrated their appreciation to the other architects of the compromise: Douglas, Foote, Cass, Cobb, Boyd, and others, who were cheered, serenaded, applauded, and extolled at their private residences.

Actually the compromise was not complete. Both houses had to reconcile minor differences in their respective bills and take up the remaining parts of Clay's original plan. On Monday, September 9, the Senate approved the House's "little omnibus," and three days later the House passed the fugitive slave bill by a vote of 109 to 76. On September 16, following the action of the Senate, the House enacted the prohibition of the slave trade in the District of Columbia, 124 to 59.[15] Fillmore immediately signed the bills as they came to him, and on September 20, the Compromise of 1850 was now the law of the land.

Later, the Nashville Convention reconvened as scheduled and the members accepted the compromise, even though only the fugitive slave law met their total approbation. The delegates adjourned without taking any further action, and the nation let out a sigh of relief.

———

Passage of the Compromise of 1850 came about because a majority of Americans demanded it. Only a minority of them opposed a settlement. "The Free Soils & disun[ion]ists & the administration of Gen'l Taylor," declared Douglas, constituted that minority. They and they alone labored to destroy any chance of resolving the conflict.[16]

Ironically, although in the Senate the omnibus could never have passed as a single package, presenting the omnibus bill really was essential to the final passage of the Compromise of 1850 in the upper house. For one thing, the omnibus, as a package, provided the surest protection against a presidential veto while Taylor was still alive. Once that threat was removed with the elevation of Millard Fillmore, it made more sense to bring each bill to the floor separately and allow senators to pick and choose which ones to support. Moreover, the omnibus brought over southern support and allowed for the creation of the Committee of Thirteen. And that committee played a vital role in providing a forum for an intense analysis and discussion of all the elements in the dispute before shaping it into a single legislative program which could then be turned over to the Senate for action.

The solution required many months of debate in the upper house before any voting could begin. And that debate took place, thanks in large measure to the efforts of Henry Clay. The individual bills could never have passed without each one being aired and analyzed and argued over for as long as necessary. The role Clay played in the final compromise required months of deliberation so that Douglas could, in the end, manage the passage of each part of the package. The final success of the Compromise of 1850 depended in the beginning on the omnibus strategy, and in the end on the individual approach. One or the other could not succeed by itself.

Clay's failure to win approval for the omnibus, aside from the impossibility of the strategy itself, was due in large part to his own lack of leadership. He quarreled with some members; annoyed, exasperated, and irritated others; and applied constant pressure on all his colleagues for a favorable vote. He succeeded in obtaining the postponement of other legislative business and thereby lengthening the workday during a period of excessive heat and humidity—none of which the members appreciated. And his attitude offended both friend and foe. He was frequently sanctimonious. He took a very patriotic and moralistic tone, implying that those who disagreed with him were lacking in patriotism or ethical behavior. Both abolitionists and Ultras were deeply offended. Clay's "want of temper," as Webster commented, his "severe morality," his frequent irritability, his overbearing manner, his interminable ranting about what would happen to the nation if secession occurred (delivered frequently "with ponderous force"), and his regular invocation "of the Deity" to attest to the justice of his cause—all these contributed to the failure of leadership that drove off needed support for the omnibus.[17]

It was so unlike him. It contradicted his great talent as a leader that had been so valuable to the nation in the past. But he was old and sick and impatient. He was intolerant of younger men daring to differ with him. And his pride got in the way. Upon his return to Congress on December 1, 1849, in a not too subtle manner, he had signaled his intent to seize leadership of the legislative process and that of the Whig Party, something that infuriated President Taylor and his friends and stiffened their determination to kill the compromise. "If Mr Clays name had not been associated with the Bills," said Douglas, "they would have passed long ago. The administration were jealous of him & hated him & some democrats were weak enough to fear that the success of the Bill would make him President."[18]

Despite his many failings, Henry Clay deserves enormous credit for putting together a package that sufficiently satisfied both sides in the controversy. He not only linked them together, but led the debate that explained the linkage and the necessity of keeping them together; he set the agenda; and he organized and conducted the meetings of supporters to generate popular approval. He tried and succeeded in exploring every conceivable avenue that could lead to success. "Let it always be said of old Hal," Douglas declared, "that he fought a glorious & a patriotic battle. No man was ever governed by higher & purer motives."[19]

And when the omnibus failed, Clay walked away. He no longer had the strength to fight on. He did not stay to figure out what went wrong and what needed to be done to reverse the decision. He left the Senate to go sunbathing in Rhode Island. He abandoned his post—which is understandable given his shattered health and pride—and left it to Stephen Douglas to repair the broken omnibus and achieve the victory that spared the Union possible civil war.

Both men received extravagant praise from the American people—and deservedly so. Douglas was spoken of as a presidential contender, and his political leadership was now confirmed.

As for Clay, the days when he might vie for the presidency had long passed. He had only two more years to live. But he was long remembered for his statesmanship in protecting the Union. Twenty-five years later, Senator Foote explained what the loss of Henry Clay had cost the nation. "Had there been one such man in the Congress of the United States as Henry Clay in 1860–61," he wrote, "there would, I feel sure, have been no civil war."[20]

EPILOGUE
Aftermath

The Compromise of 1850 is one of the most important events in the history of the United States. The mounting political struggle over slavery in the southern states had split the nation into two separate and distinct sections, each determined to prevail as the argument intensified. By 1850 the anger, bitterness, and resentment had finally become so rancorous that it appeared likely that the nation would descend into secession and civil war. Indeed, the southern states met in convention in Nashville, Tennessee, to take action, but they waited to see if the politicians in Washington could work out a compromise that would allow them to remain in the Union.

The resulting Compromise of 1850 delayed the catastrophe of civil war for ten years, and those ten years were absolutely essential for preserving the American nation under the Constitution. Had secession occurred in 1850, the South unquestionably would have made good its independence, and the country might well have split permanently into two nations. Whether further splits would have occurred in succeeding years is very likely but impossible to predict. Even ten years later, when war finally did break out, the South almost succeeded militarily in establishing its independence. Why it failed was largely due to the Compromise of 1850.

That compromise did two things that made the difference. First, it gave the North ten years to further its industrialization, by which it strengthened its ability to survive a protracted military conflict. The South did not have that capacity. It did not have the railroad system by which to move men and material to the areas where they were most needed. It did not have the factories or industries by which it could indefinitely sustain a fighting army and a functioning government. Second, the compromise gave the North ten years to find a statesman who would provide the wisdom and leadership the Union needed to successfully fight a war and pin the nation back together again. It gave the North ten years to find Abraham Lincoln. By the 1850s, after the deaths of John C. Calhoun, Henry Clay, and Daniel Webster, leadership of the nation had been reduced to such figures as presidents Millard Fillmore, Franklin Pierce, and James Buchanan, not one of whom had the talent, the skill, or the intelligence to prevent secession and civil war. By the end of the decade, Lincoln had appeared, and had shown such ability as to win the presidency in 1860 and then go on to save the Union.

Also pivotal to the success of the Compromise of 1850 was the young senator from Illinois, Stephen A. Douglas. Unfortunately, he went on to broker the Kansas-Nebraska Act in 1853, which declared the Missouri Compromise "inoperable" and divided the remaining territory of the Louisiana Purchase into two segments, Nebraska to the north and Kansas to the south. This permitted the South to insist on its right to introduce slavery into the southern portion of the territory. "I passed the Kansas-Nebraska Act," Douglas boasted. "I had the authority and power of a dictator throughout the whole controversy in both houses. The speeches were nothing. It was the marshaling and directing of men, and guarding from attacks, and with a ceaseless vigilance preventing surprise." But in the House of Representatives, Alexander H. Stephens of Georgia claimed credit: "If I had not been here the bill would never have got through. I took the reins in my hand and drove with whip & spur until we got the 'wagon out of the mud.'"[1]

Fighting broke out in Kansas over the introduction of slavery, and "Bleeding Kansas" became a tragic signal of where the nation was headed.

In 1860, the Democratic Party nominated Douglas for the presidency, and a new party, the Republican Party, named Abraham Lincoln. Southerners walked out of the Democratic convention and nominated John Breckinridge of Kentucky. Remnants of the Whig Party chose John Bell of Tennessee, and this four-way race ended with Lincoln's election. Douglas placed fourth in electoral votes but second behind Lincoln in popular votes.

Douglas had helped to spare the nation the catastrophe of civil war in 1850; now, in 1860, as one southern state after another seceded, it fell to President Lincoln to restore the Union, and it took four years of bloody conflict.

If only Henry Clay had been alive.

NOTES

CHAPTER 1

1. *Annals of Congress*, 15th Cong., 2nd sess., p. 1204.

2. Speech on December 21, 1816, in Henry Clay, *The Papers of Henry Clay*, vol. 2, *The Rising Statesman, 1815–1820*, edited by James F. Hopkins and Mary W. Hargreaves, (Lexington, KY, 1959), 263–264.

3. Henry Clay to Adam Beatty, January 22, 1820, and Henry Clay to Leslie Combs, February 5, 1820, in Clay, *Papers*, 2:766, 2:774.

4. Robert V. Remini, *Henry Clay, Statesman for the Union* (New York, 1991), 182.

5. *New York Daily Advertiser*, April 18, 1820.

6. The most recent study of the Missouri Compromise is Robert Pierce Forbes, *The Missouri Compromise and Its Aftermath: Slavery and the Meaning of America* (Chapel Hill, NC, 2007).

7. *Annals of Congress*, 16th Cong., 2nd sess., 1078–1080, 1093–1094.

8. Langdon Cheves to Henry Clay, March 3, 1821, in Henry Clay, *The Papers of Henry Clay*, vol. 3, *Presidential Candidate, 1821–1824*, edited by James F. Hopkins (Lexington, KY, 1963), 58.

9. Thomas Jefferson to John Holmes, April 22, 1820, in *The Writings of Thomas Jefferson*, vol. 10, *1816–1826*, edited by Paul Leicester Ford (New York, 1899), 157.

10. Robert V. Remini, *The Jacksonian Era* (Arlington Heights, IL, 1989), 57.

11. *Washington Globe*, August 19, 1835; Gerald S. Henig, "The Jacksonian Attitude Toward Abolitionism in the 1830s," *Tennessee Historical Quarterly* 28 (1969): 42–56.

12. Silas Wright Jr. to Azariah C. Flagg, December 18, 1827, Flagg Papers, New York Public Library (emphasis in original).

13. H. Niles to John W. Taylor, February 14, 1828, in Taylor Papers, New York Historical Society.

14. Daniel Webster to Peleg Sprague, April 13, 1828, in Daniel Webster, *The Letters of Daniel Webster*, edited by C. H. Van Tyne (New York, 1902), 135–136 (emphasis in original).

15. *Register of Debates*, 20th Cong., 1st sess., 43–80 (emphasis in original).

16. *State Papers on Nullification* (Boston, 1834), 29–31.

17. J. D. Richardson, *Compilation of the Messages and Papers of the Presidents*, vol. 2 (Washington, D.C., 1908), 1215–1219 (emphasis in original).

18. Richard Rush to Edward Livingston, December 18 and 19, 1832, Livingston Papers, Princeton University Library.

19. Joel Poinsett to Andrew Jackson, November 24, 25, and 29, 1832, Jackson Papers, Library of Congress; Jackson to Poinsett, December 2, 1832, and January 24, 1833, Poinsett Papers, Historical Society of Pennsylvania, Philadelphia, Pennsylvania.

20. Andrew Jackson to John Coffee, December 14, 1832, Coffee Papers, Tennessee Historical Society; Jackson to Lewis Cass, December 17, 1832, and January 7, 1833, and Jackson to Martin Van Buren, December 15, 1832, Jackson Papers, Library of Congress.

21. *State Papers on Nullification*, 184–201; James O'Hanlon to Andrew Jackson, December 20, 1832, Jackson Papers, Library of Congress; James Parton, *The Life of Andrew Jackson*, vol. 3 (Boston, 1866), 472.

22. Andrew Jackson to Martin Van Buren, January 13, 1833, Van Buren Papers, Library of Congress; *Washington Globe*, March 2, 1833.

23. Andrew Jackson to Francis P. Blair, August 12, 1841, Jackson Papers, Library of Congress.

24. Richardson, *Messages and Papers*, 2:1195.

25. House of Representatives, *Report*, No. 14, 22nd Cong., 2nd sess., 21.

26. Draft proposal in Daniel Webster to Hiram Ketchum, January 20, 1838, in Daniel Webster, *The Papers of Daniel Webster: Correspondence*, vol. 4, *1835–1839*, edited by Charles M. Wiltse and Harold D. Moser (Hanover, NH, 1980), 263–264.

27. John Tyler to John Floyd, January 10, 1833, Floyd Papers, Library of Congress.

28. Ibid. (emphasis in original).

29. Henry Clay to Peter B. Porter, January 29, 1833, in Henry Clay, *The Papers of Henry Clay*, vol. 8, *Candidate, Compromiser, Whig: March 5, 1829–December 31, 1836*, edited by Mary W. Hargreaves, Robert Seager, James F. Hopkins, and Melba Porter Hay (Lexington, KY, 1973), 617.

30. *Register of Debates*, 22nd Cong., 2nd sess., 100–103.

31. Andrew Jackson to Joel Poinsett, January 16, 1833, Poinsett Papers, Historical Society of Pennsylvania, Philadelphia.

32. *Register of Debates*, 22nd Cong., 2nd sess., 519–553.

33. Ibid., 537–550.

34. Silas Wright Jr. to Azariah C. Flagg, January 14 and February 2, 1833, Flagg Papers, New York Public Library.

35. Draft of compromise tariff bill in Clay, *Papers*, 8:619–620.

36. Henry Clay, *The Works of Henry Clay*, vol. 5 (New York, 1857), 537–550.

37. William Hammet to Thomas W. White, February 12, 1833, Hammet Papers, Virginia Historical Society, Richmond.

38. John Quincy Adams, *Memoirs*, vol. 8 (Philadelphia, 1874–1877), 527.

39. *Register of Debates*, 22nd Cong., 2nd sess., 715–716, 694–716.

40. Remini, *Clay*, 534–535.

41. Andrew Jackson to Reverend Andrew J. Crawford, May 1, 1833, in Andrew Jackson, *Correspondence of Andrew Jackson*, vol. 5, 1833–1838, edited by John Spencer Bassett (Washington, DC, 1929), 72.

42. Andrew Jackson to General James Winchester, October 4, 1806, Jackson, Papers, Library of Congress, 111.

43. Quoted in Remini, *Jacksonian Era*, 109.

44. *Congressional Globe*, 29th Cong., 1st sess., 1217.

CHAPTER 2

1. Henry Clay to Charles Fenton Mercer, December 10, 1848, in Henry Clay, *The Papers of Henry Clay*, vol. 10, *Candidate, Compromiser, Elder Statesman: January 1, 1844–June 29, 1852*, edited by Melba Porter Hay (Lexington, KY, 1991), 561–562.

2. Ibid.; Henry Clay to James Hughes, December 16, 1848, in Clay, *Papers*, 10:563.

3. Henry Clay to Thomas B. Stevenson, January 31, 1849, in Clay, *Papers*, 10:568 (emphasis in original).

4. Holman Hamilton, *Zachary Taylor*, vol. 2, *Soldier in the White House* (Indianapolis, 1951), 21.

5. Ibid., 2:141.

6. John Sloane to Henry Clay, February 12, 1849, in Clay, *Papers*, 10:570.

7. Henry Clay to Joseph R. Underwood, February 11, 1849, in Clay, *Papers*, 10:569–570.

8. Henry Clay to Richard Pindell, February 17, 1849, in Henry Clay, *The Works of Henry Clay*, vol. 3 (New York, 1857), 346–352.

9. Ibid.

10. *National Intelligencer*, July 4, 1849; Henry Clay to Edward Coles, June 15, 1849, in Clay, *Papers*, 10:601–602.

11. William Lloyd Garrison to Henry Clay, March 16, 1849, in Clay, *Papers*, 10:584–585.

12. Henry Clay to James Brown Clay, March 3, 1849, in Clay, *Papers*, 10:582.

13. Henry Clay to Christopher Hughes, August 4, 1849, in Clay, *Papers*, 10:609.

14. Ibid.

15. Philip Hone, *The Diary of Philip Hone*, vol. 2, *1828–1851*, edited by Allan Nevins (New York, 1927), 877; Henry Clay to Mr. and Mrs. Frederick Hollister, September 19, 1849, in Clay, *Papers*, 10:617.

16. Benjamin Brown French said he had no doubt that Clay had been and was still the most popular man in America. French, *Witness to the Young Republic: A Yankee's Journal, 1828–1870*, edited by Donald B. Cole and John J. McDonough (Hanover, NH, 1989), 213.

17. Jefferson was Washington's secretary of state, Madison was Jefferson's secretary of state, Monroe was Madison's secretary of state, and John Quincy Adams was Monroe's secretary of state.

18. Henry Clay to James W. Simonton, February 8, 1850, in Clay, *Papers*, 10:673.

19. Margaret Bayard Smith, *The First Forty Years of Washington Society Portrayed by the Family Letters of Mrs. Samuel Harrison Smith*, edited by Gaillard Hunt (New York, 1906), 285–286.

20. Henry Clay to John C. Vaughan and Tomas Brown, June 16, 1849, in Clay, *Papers*, 10:603.

21. *Lexington Observer and Kentucky Reporter*, December 5, 1849.

22. Henry Clay to John G. Pound et al., November 26, 1849, in Clay, *Papers*, 10:627–628.

23. *Lexington Observer and Kentucky Reporter*, December 5, 1849.

24. French, *Witness to the Young Republic*, 213.

25. Edgar De Witt Jones, *The Influence of Henry Clay on Abraham Lincoln* (Lexington, KY, 1952), 21.

26. Henry Clay to Thomas B. Stevenson, December 21, 1849, in Clay, *Papers*, 10:635.

27. Benjamin Perley Poore, *Perley's Reminiscences of Sixty Years in the National Metropolis*, vol. 1 (Philadelphia, 1886), 363.

28. Henry Clay to Mary S. Bayard, December 14, 1849, in Clay, *Papers*, 10:633.

29. Henry Clay to Robert S. Hamilton, October 2, 1849, in Clay, *Papers*, 10:621.

30. Holman Hamilton, *Prologue to Conflict: The Crisis and Compromise of 1850* (New York, 1966), 40.

31. John W. Forney, *Anecdotes of Public Men*, vol. 1, (New York, 1970), 57, 165.

32. *Congressional Globe*, 31st Cong., 2nd sess., 28 (emphasis in original).

33. Quoted in Michael Holt, *The Rise and Fall of the American Whig Party* (New York, 1999), 467–468.

34. Nathan Sargent, *Public Men and Events*, vol. 2 (Philadelphia, 1875), 351.

35. *Congressional Globe*, 31st Cong., 1st sess., 256, 351.

36. Ibid., 451–455.

37. Avery Craven, *The Coming of the Civil War* (New York, 1942), 242–244.

38. Quoted in Thelma Jennings, *The Nashville Convention: Southern Movement for Unity, 1848–1851* (Memphis, 1980), 39 (emphasis in original).

39. Ibid., 36.

40. Ibid., 7.

41. Clay, *Papers*, 10:636.

42. *Lexington Observer and Kentucky Reporter*, February 9 and 23, 1850, and March 16, 1850.

43. Henry Clay to James Brown Clay, January 2, 1850, in Clay, *Papers*, 10:642.

44. Elbert B. Smith, *The Presidencies of Zachary Taylor and Millard Fillmore* (Lawrence, KS, 1988), 95–101; Hamilton, *Prologue to Conflict*, 17–21; Michael F. Holt, *Political Crises of the 1850s* (New York, 1978), 77–78; Allan Nevins, *Ordeal of the Union*, vol. 1 (New York, 1958), 257.

45. William Cooper Jr., *The South and the Politics of Slavery, 1828–1856* (Baton Rouge, 1978), 290–295; *Congressional Globe*, 31st Cong., 1st sess., 27–28 (emphasis in original).

CHAPTER 3

1. Daniel Webster to Franklin Haven, January 13, 1850, in Daniel Webster, *The Papers of Daniel Webster*, vol. 7, *Correspondence: 1850–1852*, edited by Charles M. Wiltse and Michael J. Birkner (Hanover, NH, 1986), 5.

2. For a defense of Taylor's plan see Elbert B. Smith, *The Presidencies of Zachary Taylor and Millard Fillmore* (Lawrence, KS, 1988), 91–122. Daniel Walker Howe also regards the president's plan as "straightforward and statesmanlike," and not pro-slavery. Daniel Walker Howe, *The Political Culture of the American Whigs* (Chicago, 1979), 146–147.

3. Henry Clay to Lucretia Hart Clay, January 11, 1850, in Henry Clay, *The Papers of Henry Clay*, vol. 10, *Candidate, Compromiser, Elder Statesman: January 1, 1844–June 29, 1852*, edited by Melba Porter Hay (Lexington, KY, 1991), 647.

4. George Ticknor Curtis, *Life of Daniel Webster*, vol. 2, (New York, 1870), 397–398.

5. Henry Clay to James Harlan, January 24, 1850, in Clay, *Papers*, 10:653.

6. Henry Clay to Boyd McNairy, January 26, 1850, in Clay, *Papers*, 10:654.

7. *Congressional Globe*, 31st Cong., 1st sess., Appendix, 115–127

8. Henry B. Stanton, *Random Recollections* (New York, 1887), 151.

9. Breese to Webster, in Webster, *Papers*, 7:34.

10. George Ticknor Curtis, *Life of Daniel Webster*, vol. 2 (New York, 1870), 397–398.

11. *Congressional Globe*, 31st Cong., 1st sess., 399–405.

12. Ibid., 244.

13. Ibid., 244–252.

14. Ibid.

15. Henry Clay to Daniel Ullmann, February 2, 1850, in Clay, *Papers*, 10:660; Philip Hone, *The Diary of Philip Hone*, vol. 2, *1828–1851*, edited by Allan Nevins (New York, 1927), 885.

16. Quoted in Holman Hamilton, *Prologue to Conflict: The Crisis and Compromise of 1850* (Lexington, KY, 1966), 56.

17. *Congressional Globe*, 31st Cong., 1st sess., Appendix, 115–127.

18. Henry Clay to Lucretia Clay, February 7, 1850, in Clay, *Papers*, 10:672.

19. Martin Van Buren to Francis P. Blair, February 9, 1850, Blair Papers, Library of Congress.

20. *New York Herald*, November 21, 1850.

21. *Frankfort Commonwealth*, December 16, 1851.

22. Quoted in Hamilton, *Prologue to Conflict*, 60, 68.

23. *New York Herald*, February 12, 17, 18, 19, 23, 26, 1850.

24. Hone, *Diary*, 2:885; *National Intelligencer*, February 17, 1850; *New York Herald*, February 26, 1850; *Congressional Globe*, 31st Cong., 1st sess., 1107, 1139–1142, 1202–1203, 1263–1264.

25. James Ford Rhodes, *History of the United States Since the Compromise of 1850*, vol. 1, (New York, 1902), 173n; *National Intelligencer*, November 17, 1850.

26. Hamilton, *Prologue to Conflict*, 63.

27. Ibid., 63–64.

28. *Congressional Globe*, 31st Cong., 1st sess., Appendix, 149–155.

29. Ibid., 202–206.

30. Quoted in Hamilton, *Prologue to Conflict*, 66.

31. Alexander H. Stephens, *A Constitutional View of the Late War Between the States*, vol. 2, (Philadelphia, 1868–1870), 202–204.

32. *Congressional Globe*, 31st Cong., 1st sess., 375–385.

33. Ibid., 656–657.

34. Ibid., 660–661.

35. Mary Mann, *Life of Horace Mann* (Boston, 1891), 292–293.

36. *Congressional Globe*, 31st Cong., 1st sess., 353–355, 365–369, 399–405 (emphasis in original).

CHAPTER 4

1. *Congressional Globe*, 31st Cong., 1st sess., 451–455.

2. Holman Hamilton, *Prologue to Conflict: The Crisis and Compromise of 1850* (Lexington, KY, 1966), 74.

3. Robert Winthrop Jr., *A Memoir of Robert C. Winthrop* (Boston, 1897), 110, 111; Robert Winthrop Jr. to Edward Everett, March 3, 1850, Everett Papers, Massachusetts Historical Society.

4. Daniel Webster to Fletcher Webster, February 24, 1850, in Daniel Webster, *The Papers of Daniel Webster: Correspondence*, vol. 7, *1850–1852*, edited by Charles M. Wiltse and Michael J. Birkner (Hanover, 1986), 16.

5. Daniel Webster to Peter Harvey, [March 1, 1850], in Webster, *Papers*, 7:19.

6. Daniel Webster to Charles Henry Warren, March 1, 1850, in *The Writings and Speeches of Daniel Webster*, vol. 16, (Boston, 1903), 535.

7. Benjamin Silliman to Daniel Webster, March 5, 1850, and R. B. Barker to Daniel Webster, March 4, 1850, in Webster, *Papers*, 7:21, 22.

8. Waddy Hampson to Daniel Webster, March 2, 1850, in Webster, *Papers*, 7:21.

9. Daniel Webster to Peter Harvey, April 7, 1850, in Webster, *Papers*, 7:54.

10. Winthrop, *Memoir*, 111–112.

11. *Congressional Globe*, 31st Cong., 1st sess., 476.

12. Ibid., 476–483.

13. Samuel P. Lyman, *Public and Private Life of Daniel Webster*, vol. 2, (Philadelphia, 1852), 158.

14. Philip Hone, *The Diary of Philip Hone*, vol. 2, *1828–1851*, edited by Allan Nevins (New York, 1927), 887.

15. See *National Intelligencer*, March 9 and 19, 1850.

16. Daniel Webster to George Ticknor, March 17, 1851, in Daniel Webster, *Writings & Speeches*, vol. 18 (Boston, 1903), 359.

17. Theodore Parker, *The Collected Works of Theodore Parker*, edited by Frances Power Cobbe (London, 1863), 228, 231; Ralph Waldo Emerson,

Works, vol. 11, 181; John Greenleaf Whittier, *The Complete Poetical Works of John Greenleaf Whittier* (New York, 1894), 186.

18. John C. Calhoun to James H. Hammond, February 16, 1850, and John C. Calhoun to Thomas G. Clemens, March 10, 1850, in John C. Calhoun, *Correspondence of John C. Calhoun*, vol. 2, edited by J. Franklin Jameson [1900], 781, 784.

19. *Congressional Globe*, 31st Cong., 1st sess., Appendix, 260–269.

CHAPTER 5

1. *Congressional Globe*, 31st Cong., 1st sess., Appendix, 262–265.

2. Holman Hamilton, *Prologue to Conflict: The Crisis and Compromise of 1850* (New York, 1966), 85–86.

3. *Congressional Globe*, 31st Cong., 1st sess., Appendix, 364–375.

4. Robert W. Johannsen, *Stephen A. Douglas* (New York, 1973), 79.

5. *Congressional Globe*, 31st Cong., 1st sess., Appendix, 468–480.

6. Henry Clay to James Harlan, March 16, 1850, and Henry Clay to Thomas B. Stevenson, April 3, 1850, in Henry Clay, *The Works of Henry Clay*, vol. 4 (New York, 1857), 603–604.

7. Allan Nevins, *Ordeal of the Union*, vol. 1, *Fruits of Manifest Destiny: 1847–1852* (New York, 1947), 501–502.

8. *Congressional Globe*, 31st Cong., 1st sess., 510, and Appendix, 364–375.

9. Ibid., 760–763.

10. *National Intelligencer*, April 15, 1850.

11. *Congressional Globe*, 31st Cong., 1st sess., 781.

12. Stephen A. Douglas to Charles H. Lamphier and George Walker, in Stephen A. Douglas, *The Letters of Stephen A. Douglas*, edited by Robert W. Johannsen (Urbana, IL, 1961), 191.

13. *Congressional Globe*, 31st Cong., 1st sess., 948–950; Henry Clay to Lucretia Clay, April 25, 1850, Thomas J. Clay Papers, Library of Congress.

14. *Congressional Globe*, 31st Cong., 1st sess., pp. 944–950.

15. Ibid.

16. Clay, *Works*, vol. 6, 426–451.

17. *Congressional Globe*, 31st Cong., 1st sess., Appendix, 867.

18. Hamilton, *Prologue to Conflict*, 98–99.

19. Ibid., 100–101.

20. *Congressional Globe*, 31st Cong., 1st sess., 1005.

21. Ibid., Appendix, 612–616, 897–899, 902–903.

22. The "five wounds" were the issues of California, New Mexico, the Texas boundary, fugitive slaves, and slavery in the District.

23. Henry Clay, *The Papers of Henry Clay*, vol. 10, *Candidate, Compromiser, Elder Statesman: January 1, 1844–June 29, 1852*, edited by Melba Porter Hay (Lexington, KY, 1991), 728–730.

24. Daniel Webster to Moses Stuart, May 30, 1850, in Daniel Webster, *The Papers of Daniel Webster*, vol. 7, *Correspondence, 1850–1852*, edited by Charles M. Wiltse and Michael J. Birkner (Hanover, NH, 1986), 105.

25. Henry Clay to Thomas Hart Clay, May 31, 1850, in Clay, *Papers*, 10:736.

26. Thelma Jennings, *The Nashville Convention: Southern Movement for Unity, 1848–1851* (Memphis, 1980), 137, 106-107.

27. Quoted in ibid., 140.

28. Henry Clay to Lucretia Clay, July 6, 1850, in Clay, *Papers*, 10:763.

29. Willie P. Mangum to Charity A. Mangum, July 10, 1850, in Willie P. Mangum, *Willie Mangum Papers*, vol. 5 (Raleigh, NC: 1950–1956), 181. Mangum did not believe cabbages and cucumbers were fit for "Bipeds."

30. Henry Clay to James Clay, July 18, 1850, in Clay, *Papers*, 10:767.

31. *Congressional Globe*, 31st Cong., 1st sess., Appendix, 306, 1473; Johannsen, *Douglas*, 292; Robert J. Rayback, *Millard Fillmore: Biography of a President* (Buffalo, NY, 1959), 242–247.

32. Quoted in Robert V. Remini, *Clay: Statesman for the Union* (New York, 1991), 754.

33. Clay, *Papers*, 10:772–783; *Congressional Globe*, 31st Cong., 1st sess., Appendix, 1405–1415.

34. *National Intelligencer*, July 23, 1850.

35. Grace Greenwood, letter of July 25, 1850, in *Greenwood Leaves: A Collection of Sketches and Letters* (Boston, 1852), 328.

36. *Congressional Globe*, 31st Cong., 1st sess., Appendix, 1449, 1458–1459, 1473–1474

37. Quoted in George Rawlings Poage, *Henry Clay and the Whig Party* (Chapel Hill, NC, 1936), 157.

38. *Congressional Globe*, 31st Cong., 1st sess., 1504, Appendix, 1482–1485; Remini, *Clay*, 756–757; *National Intelligencer*, August 1, 1850.

39. Stephen A. Douglas to Charles H. Lamphire and George Walker, August 3, 1850, in Douglas, *Letters*, 191.

40. *National Intelligencer*, August 6, 1850.

CHAPTER 6

1. Henry Clay to John R. Thomson, August 14, 1850, in Henry Clay, *The Papers of Henry Clay*, vol. 10, *Candidate, Compromiser, Elder Statesman: January 1, 1844–June 29, 1852*, edited by Melba Porter Hay (Lexington, KY, 1991), 793–794.

2. Quoted in Holman Hamilton, *Prologue to Conflict: The Crisis and Compromise of 1850* (New York, 1966), 136.

3. *Congressional Globe*, 31st Cong., 1st sess., 1573, 1589, 1647, 1660.

4. Hamilton, *Prologue to Conflict*, 141.

5. Holman Hamilton, "Democratic Senate Leadership and the Compromise of 1850," *Mississippi Valley Historical Review* 41 (December 1954): 407–412.

6. Hamilton, *Prologue to Conflict*, 143.

7. Robert W. Johannsen, *Stephen A. Douglas* (New York, 1973), 296.

8. Speech by Stephen A. Douglas on September 20, 1850, in James Ford Rhodes, *History of the United States from the Compromise of 1850 to the McKinley-Bryan Campaign of 1896*, vol. 1, *1850–1854* (New York, 1896), 173n.

9. Hamilton, *Prologue to Conflict*, 148.

10. Quoted in Johannsen, *Douglas*, 296–297.

11. *Congressional Globe*, 31st Cong., 1st sess., 1695–1704.

12. By definition, the engrossment of a bill is the formal reprinting of it in the form upon which the members will vote final passage.

13. *Congressional Globe*, 31st Cong., 1st sess., 1764.

14. Hamilton, *Prologue to Conflict*, 161.

15. *Congressional Globe*, 31st Cong., 1st sess., 1784, 1806–1807.

16. Stephen A. Douglas to Charles H. Lamphier and George Walker, August 3, 1850, in Stephen A. Douglas, *The Letters of Douglas*, edited by Robert W. Johannsen (Urbana, IL, 1961), 191.

17. Daniel Webster to Franklin Haven, July 4, 1850, in Daniel Webster, *The Papers of Daniel Webster*, vol. 7, *Correspondence: 1850–1852*, edited by Charles M. Wiltse and Michael J. Birkner (Hanover, NH, 1986), 121.

18. Douglas to Lamphire and Walker, August 3, 1850, in Douglas, *Letters*, 192–193.

19. Ibid.

20. Henry Foote, *Casket of Reminiscences* (reprint, New York, 1968), 30.

EPILOGUE

1. Quoted in Robert V. Remini, *A Short History of the United States* (New York, 2008), 136.

Index

death of, ix, 108–109, 119, 158
health of, 64, 91, 98, 99, 100
and slavery, 55, 64, 70, 83, 91–
96, 97, 98, 99, 106, 120
and southern unity, 54–55
and tariffs and nullification, 13,
23–27
California
acquisition of, 33, 38, 41
admission into Union of, x, 41,
59, 60, 65, 71, 75, 85, 86, 87,
89, 99, 106, 112, 113, 114,
115, 116–118, 119–120, 123,
124, 125, 127, 128, 137, 144–
146
and gold, 58, 112
and Polk, 31
and slavery and omnibus, 46,
47, 52, 58–59, 60, 67, 71, 75,
79, 85, 86, 93, 101, 112, 116–
118, 124, 125, 127–128, 129,
137, 140, 144–146, 151
Calvert, Charles Benedict, 123,
151
Campbell, Thomas Jefferson, 53
Canada, 31
Cass, Lewis, 50, 64
and 1848 election, 34
and slavery and omnibus, 83,
122, 123, 144, 147, 148, 149,
151
and tariffs, 16
Charleston Mercury (newspaper),
107
Chase, Salmon P., 50, 64, 81, 115
Cheves, Langdon, 8
Cincinnati Daily Atlas
(newspaper), 42

Clay, Henry
and Calhoun's death, 109
and "corrupt bargain" charge,
65, 69
death of, ix, 155, 158, 159
description and background of,
4–5
and 1848 election, 34, 37
and 1844 election, 30–31
and 1824 election, 44–45
and Fillmore, 134
health of, 43–44, 46, 49, 65,
68, 69, 123, 141, 144, 154
intellectual strength of, 45–46
lack of discipline of, 45
and Lincoln, 48–49
and Missouri, 3–4, 5, 6, 7–8,
141
and Nashville Convention, 56–
58, 132
and omnibus bill, 88, 116–117,
118–120, 123–131, 132, 134,
135–139, 140–142, 143–144,
145, 147, 148, 149, 150, 151,
153–155
popularity of, 44, 46, 47–48,
49, 122
return to Congress of, 37–40,
46, 49–51, 65, 154
sanctimoniousness, irritability,
and overbearing manner of,
153
seventy-third birthday of, 121
and slavery, 38, 39, 40–43, 46–
47, 50–51, 57, 58, 63, 65,
66–89, 97, 106–107, 108,
109, 112, 114, 115, 116–120,
121–131, 132, 134, 135–139